F.R.DAVID

"RECOGNITION"*

Edited with Scott Rogers

uh books

with

KW Institute for Contemporary Art

* cf. p. 201

P. 3

In the lower montane forests of the Eastern Highlands of Papua New Guinea, a population of some 14,000 slash-and-burn horticulturalists known as the Fore (pronounced FOR-AY) tend gardens of sweet potato, taro, yam, corn, and other vegetables. They also grow sugarcane and bananas, keep pigs, and, in the sparsely populated regions near their southern boundaries, still hunt for birds, mammals, reptiles, and cassowaries.

P. 6

The Fore are afflicted with a rare disease. Since record-keeping began in 1957, three years after the Australian administration established a patrol post at Okapa, some 2,500 people in this region have died from kuru, a subacute degenerative disorder of the central nervous system.

P. 6

When the incidence of kuru reached a peak in the 1960s, the South Fore believed their society was coming to an end.

P. 61

Kuru [South Fore diagnosis]

Symptoms: Headache, arm and leg pain. Walking becomes unstable, movements uncoordinated. Some double vision. Final immobility, derangement, refusal to eat food. Death within a period of three months to about two and a half years. Body of most kuru victims is full of grease, as with pigs.

Sorcery Method: The sorcerer steals food remnants, hair, nail clippings, or excrement from the victim. He makes a bundle with leaves and some sorcerer's stone, places the bundle in muddy ground, and names the victim. As the bundle rots, the victim exhibits symptoms.

Preface:

The discernment of humanity requires the activation of the autonomous space of reason. But since this space—qua the content of humanity— is functionally autonomous even though its genesis is historical, its activation implies the deactivation of historical anticipations of what humanity can be or become at a descriptive level. Since antihumanism mostly draws its critical power from this descriptive level either situated in nature (allegedly immune to revision) or in a restricted scope of history (based on a particular anticipation), the realization of the autonomy of reason would restore the nontheological significance of human as an initial necessary condition, thus nullifying the antihumanist critique. What is important to understand here is that one cannot defend or even speak of inhumanism without first committing to the humanist project through the front door of the Enlightenment. [*read further on p..35*]

PREFACE

"When you rub your finger on the wood, you feel the wood. If you get a splinter, you feel your finger. That's how pain works: it moves from outside to inside."ii

"IT IS WELL KNOWN that Spinoza defends a type of psycho-physical parallelism. Because mind and body are modes of a single substance rather than distinct mental and material substances, there can be no causal interaction between them. Instead, their connection is explicated as a union, which is expressed in Spinoza's claim that mind is the idea or awareness of an actually existing individual body. Mind, then, [...] is a series of ideas corresponding to the series of states [...] determined by two factors: by what the body is in itself [...] and by the influence of other bodies [or] 'the state of a body represents at each moment itself and those bodies of the surrounding world which affect it...'1

---

1. Hans Jonas, "Spinoza and the Theory of Organism" in *Spinoza: A Collection of Critical Essays*, edited by Marjorie Grene, (Garden City, New York: Anchor Books, 1973), 273.

Spinoza closely associates these two factors. The capacity of a body to be affected by external bodies is a function of the degree of complexity of its own internal organization, which is why one of the defining features of more complex and powerful bodies is a capacity for 'being acted on in many ways at once'.[2] It follows that the mind's powers of perception and thought also increase in direct proportion to its body's capacity to be affected. Thus, the ability of a particular individual, or mind-body union, to persist and thrive is directly related to its capacity for being acted on and affected by other bodies insofar as they contribute to its survival. The human body, Spinoza tells us, 'requires a great many bodies by which it is, as it were, continually regenerated.'[3]

This vital interplay between our capacity to act and be acted upon, to affect and be affected, is one of the most strikingly original aspects of Spinoza's theory of the individual. [Our] receptivity, or openness to what can affect us, is not the mark of our passivity in the face of the external forces of nature, but is itself a power, and a power which increases our power of acting. Hans Jonas suggests that through this mutual dependence of passive and active power Spinoza is able to move beyond the apparent dichotomy between self-determination and determination from without. The profundity of his

2. Benedict de Spinoza, "Ethics" in *A Spinoza Reader: The Ethics and Other Works*, edited and translated by Edwin Curley (Princeton: Princeton University Press, 1994), EIIP13S. Citations are by book and proposition number, and follow Curley's notation.
3. EIIP19Dem.

philosophy follows from this insight into the complementarity of receptivity and spontaneity, a complementarity which implies that 'only by being sensitive can life be active, only by being exposed can it be autonomous.'[4]

It is here, in this linking of our vulnerability to being affected with our capacities for agency, that we can see the potential for a productive dialogue between Spinoza's account of individuality and feminist efforts to critically revise the traditionally conflictual interpretation of the social and autonomous self. […] Spinoza's theory of *conatus* explains what it means to exist as the inherent striving of the individual to maintain identity in and through […] exchanges with its environment. Thus it makes no sense for Spinoza to think of the individual in isolation from its world – what it affects and is affected by, what it seeks and avoids, what strengthens or threatens it. Just as each state of the body reflects both itself and those other bodies which affect it, so the activity of the mind reflects both its body object and its interactions with the world. This expansion of the boundaries of individuality to encompass cognitive and corporeal relations with the environment, combined with a rejection of the transcendence of the self, implies a radical rejection of atomic assumptions about selfhood. Indeed it is hard to overestimate how far Spinoza has moved from Descartes' conception of the individual as a *res cogitans*, an isolated consciousness which is separate from the body and set over against the world it apprehends. […]

---

4. Jonas, p.278.

PREFACE

In part three of his *Ethics* Spinoza analyses specific emotions in terms of [the] primary affects of joy and sadness, and considers these emotions in terms of the idea of their causes. It is this idea of the causes of our emotional states that Spinoza appeals to in order to explain the difference between passions and actions. Affects that are passions, he suggests, involve inadequate ideas, that is, ideas which are confused insofar as they reflect awareness of the state of my own body mixed together with awareness of external bodies impinging on it. Affects, however, cease to be passions to which we are subjected and become actions when we form an adequate idea of their causes. It is knowledge of the causes of our emotional states, rather than freedom from the affects, that is, for Spinoza, the key to active self-determination. Spinoza's version of autonomy thus involves remedying our passivity by coming to understand the causes of our emotions and actions. We become more autonomous when more of what we do and feel can be understood through our nature alone; that is, with reference to our own power, rather than the power of external causes.[5] And we become the adequate cause of what we do when we understand the sources of our appetites, motivations and emotions and how they function in our current situation. Amelie Rorty describes this as a process in which 'the mind acknowledges and absorbs as constitutive of its nature, the determinative causal line that had seemed "external" to it.'[6]

---

5 EIVP59Dem.

6. Amelie Oksenberg Rorty, "The Two Faces of Spinoza", *Review of Metaphysics* 41 (1987):300.

PREFACE

To the extent that we understand something, it ceases to be "outside" us. Understanding the causal determinations of our actions, through a gradual articulation of the determinants of our ideas and affects, is the transition from relative passivity to increased activity. Thus, for Spinoza, freedom is a function of adequate knowledge of oneself and one's emotions.

There are, however, necessary limits to our self-knowledge and activity. It is impossible, Spinoza tells us, 'that a man should not be a part of Nature, and that he should be able to undergo no changes except those which can be understood through his own nature alone, and of which he is the adequate cause.'[7]

Spinoza's account of activity as a function of adequate beliefs about our selves and our emotions contains clear parallels with more modern theories of autonomy. The notion of activity as self-causation can be linked to notions of self-determination and self-direction, and the focus on the adequacy of our ideas evokes the requirements for self-knowledge and rational reflection which are central to many accounts of autonomy.[8] These obvious parallels, however, need to be carefully qualified. If we recall that, for Spinoza, the mark of more complex and powerful individuals is a heightened capacity to be acted on and affected by other bodies, and that the mind's power to think and, therefore,

---

7. EIVP4.
8. For an insightful discussion of the parallels between modern theories of autonomy and Spinoza's account of activity and freedom, see Douglas Den Uyl, "Autonomous Autonomy: Spinoza on Autonomy, Perfectionism, and Politics", *Social Philosophy and Policy*, Vol. 20, no. 2 (Summer 2003): 30–69.

PREFACE

to form adequate ideas, increases in proportion to its body's capacity to be acted on, then we cannot understand Spinoza's version of self-determination to imply freedom from determination. Spinoza famously rejects Descartes' version of autonomy as a function of the will's freedom from causal determination. He must do so since he understands the details of an individual's identity to be determined by its causal history and interactions with others. Spinoza's notion of self-causation does require us to locate all the causes of our emotions within the self, but this should not be construed as a narrowing of the sphere of action to that over which the self can exert direct control. Internalizing the causes of emotions through understanding does not involve insulating the self from exposure to affection. On the contrary, the gradual effort to understand the causes of one's emotions requires attending to the complex history of one's causal and affective interactions."[iii]

Transcribed by Will Holder*

i. Portrait of the author, Aurelia Armstrong
ii. Stephen Dwoskin, *Pain Is...*, 1997, 80 minutes, Colour, Opt.
iii. Aurelia Armstrong, "Autonomy and the relational individual: Spinoza and feminism," Moira Gatens ed., *Feminist Interpretations of Spinoza* (Pennsylvania State University Press, 2009).

---

*Originally commisioned as Preface to Mason Leaver-Yap, *Mediated Monologues*, Sputnik and Fizzle, 2016. ...*for single mothers*

Offerings

UNLIKE OTHER SOCIAL SYSTEMS that derive their power from definition and structure, friendship derives its power from unstable elements. Its participants continually negotiate and regulate its shape, rules, and scope, while being able to enter or leave the field of friendship at any moment. Entrance, of course, is always consensual; exit, rarely so. But this short text is not about the termination and dissolution of friendship. It is about the denial of an ideal form in favour of relation, interdependency and sacrifice.

Amidst its many moving parts (some redundant, others typically overworked), friendship will always emerge as a sacrificial economy. Participants may engage in private forms, such as working, sleeping, eating, drinking, and the acquiring of personal belongings, to name only a few of society's most essential and fixed forms. These activities seemingly occur beyond the purview of friendship, but they are never really beyond its scope; rather, they are its offerings.

Indeed, friendship gains its symbolic value—its comfort and its privilege—from the sacrifice of such things. Sleepless nights are absorbed into the body for the benefit of late-night conversations; food and drink is split, shared and jointly consumed; work is interrupted and put on hold for the benefit of another to whom one feels close; treasured objects are given, borrowed or else accidentally destroyed, breakages are forgiven. In its pursuit of the symbolic, friendship thrives on the destruction of material things of personal worth. The destruction of value is pleasantness shared. Friendship must continue to revel in destruction to prevent stasis and atrophy.

This collapse of normal value and judgment systems is perhaps what makes friendship so prized within social systems. Forged on personal or material exhaustion, friendship necessarily sidesteps like-for-like forms of exchange. Also key is its vagueness: the benefits or rewards of friendship cannot really demand anything specific, much in the same way that a 'gift' must necessarily be given freely and without expectation in order to acquire the term 'gift' at all. But unlike the act of gifting, friendship is not a devotional form. Comprehension of personal surrender is key to the expansion and recognition of friendship; sacrifices must be acknowledged as well as offered. The give with the take produces equality between participants, and it is the witnessing and affirmation of this dynamic that makes friendship a human quality, as opposed to something that can be produced by animals.

'Between friends' is a phrase, for example, that indicates the dynamism of such dialogue. It makes and delineates space by temporarily cordoning off emotional territory that is private, conspiratorial, and mutual. The limit of the body and the individual mind are linguistically bridged in favour of a unified space. This intimate zone also indicates a transparency

or frankness that the space outside of friendship will not permit. Sharing thoughts is not simply broadcasting; it is the process of opening oneself up to challenge and rejection. Friendship, then, is the safest space to embark upon such a perilous activity.

The perception of another person is the first step of friendship; it represents the willingness to receive a human transmission, and perhaps more. The human eye—one that meets a human gaze—has the capacity to acknowledge the other, to witness and share a context. The matching of a look between two people is the soft simulation of porous body contact. I see you, I feel you. Of course, looking is never enough, but it is an acknowledgment of intersubjectivity, where intersubjectivity is the promise of friendship. Solitude is temporarily abated.

By contrast, the animal eye does not offer affirmation of the other. Its language of perception cannot be shared. Unyielding, it absorbs the indiscretions of false affinity, empathy and projection, but it also baldly presents itself as pure impasse; it solidifies and mirrors the unshared elements of the secret self. I see you, but what do you see? Its gaze reduces us to beasts. The sacrifice required for its equality is more than we are willing to offer.

Previously published in *a caelo usque ad centrum*, Dena Yago & Laurie Spiegel, Cubitt, 2014; Richard Birkett and Charlotte Linton, 2014; *A Circular*, ed. Pedro Cid Proença, 2015; *Mediated Monologues*, Mason Leaver-Yap, 2015–ongoing.

'Circus' is the collective noun for a flock of kea (*Nestor notabilis*), a parrot
species endemic to the south island of Aotearoa (New Zealand). Found at
or above treeline, kea are the only parrot living predominantly in alpine
environments. Social, collaborative, intelligent, and inquisitive, kea are known
to play with, exploit, and disrupt human systems they come in contact with.
The preceding images survey Scott Rogers' collection of objects that kea have
engaged with, in and around the Homer Tunnel in Fiordland National Park.
These objects include parts of windscreen wipers, wing mirrors,
and the viewfinder of a Nikon camera.

The Labor of the Inhuman
Part I: Human*

Inhumanism is the extended practical elaboration of humanism; it is born out of a diligent commitment to the project of enlightened humanism. As a universal wave that erases the self-portrait of man drawn in sand, inhumanism is a vector of revision. It relentlessly revises what it means to be human by removing its supposed evident characteristics and preserving certain invariances. At the same time, inhumanism registers itself as a demand for construction, to define what it means to be human by treating human as a constructible hypothesis, a space of navigation and intervention. [...]

* [footnote from Part II, see opposite] Throughout the text, the term "human" often appears without a definite article in order to emphasize its meaning as a singular universal which makes sense of its mode of being by inhabiting collectivizing or universalizing processes. This is "human" not by virtue of being a biological species, but rather by virtue of being a generic subject or a commoner before what brings about its singularity and universality. Accordingly, human, as Jean-Paul Sartre points out, is universal by the singular universality of human history, and it is also singular by the universalizing singularity of the projects it undertakes.

Previously published in *eflux Journal* #52 & #53

REZA NEGARESTANI

The Labor of the Inhuman

Part II: The Inhuman

ENLIGHTENED HUMANISM as a project of *commitment to humanity*, in the entangled sense of what it means to be human and what it means to make a commitment, is a rational project. It is rational not only because it locates the meaning of human[*] in the space of reasons as a specific horizon of practices, but also and more importantly, because the concept of commitment it adheres to cannot be thought or practiced as a voluntaristic impulse free of ramifications and growing obligations. Instead, this is commitment as a rational system for navigating collateral commitments—their ramifications as well as their specific entitlements—that result from making an initial commitment.

The contention of this essay is that universality and collectivism cannot be thought, let alone attained, through consensus or dissensus between cultural tropes, but only by intercepting and rooting out what gives rise to the economy of false choices and by activating and fully elaborating what real human significance consists of. For it is, as will be argued, the truth of human significance—not in the sense of an original meaning or a birthright, but in the sense of a labor that consists of the extended elaboration of what it means to be human through a series of upgradable special performances—that is rigorously inhuman. [...]

But what is humanism? What specific *commitment* does "being human" represent and how does the full practical elaboration of this commitment amount to *in*humanism? In other words, what is it in human that shapes the inhuman once it is developed in terms of its entitlements and consequences? In order to answer these questions, first we need to define what it means to be human and exactly what commitment "being human" endorses. Then we need to analyze the structure of this commitment in order to grasp how undertaking such a commitment—in the sense of practicing it—entails inhumanism.

Interaction with the rational system of commitments follows a navigational paradigm in which the ramifications of an initial commitment must be compulsively elaborated and navigated in order for this commitment to make sense as an undertaking. It is the examination of the rational fallout of making a commitment, the unpacking of its far-reaching consequences, and the treating of these ramifications as paths to be explored that shapes commitment to humanity as a navigational project. Here, navigation is not only a survey of a landscape whose full scope is not given; it is also an exercise in the non-monotonic procedures of steering, plotting out routes, suspending navigational preconceptions, rejecting or resolving incompatible commitments, exploring the space of possibilities, and understanding each path as a hypothesis leading to new paths or a lack thereof—transits as well as obstructions.

---

1. Commitment as Extended and Multimodal Elaboration

A commitment only makes sense by virtue of its pragmatic content (meaning through use) and its demand to adopt an intervening attitude. This attitude aims to elaborate the content of a commitment and then update that commitment according to the ramifications or collateral commitments that are made explicit in the course of elaboration. In short, a commitment—be it assertional, inferential, practical, or cognitive—can neither be examined nor properly undertaken without the process of updating the commitment and unpacking its consequences through a full range of multimodal practices. In this sense, humanism is a commitment to humanity, but only by virtue of what a commitment is and what human is combined together.

The analysis of the structure and laws of commitment-making and the meaning of being human in a pragmatic sense (i.e., not by resorting to an inherent conception of meaning hidden in nature or a predetermined idea of man) is a necessary initial step before entering the domain of making prescriptions (whether social, political, or ethical).

From a rational perspective, a commitment is seen as a cascade of ramifying paths that is in the process of expanding its frontiers, developing into an evolving landscape, unmooring its fixed perspectives, deracinating any form of rootedness associated with a fixed commitment or immutable responsibilities, revising links and addresses between its old and new commitments, and finally, erasing any image of itself as "what it was supposed to be."

To place the meaning of human in the rational system of commitments is to submit the presumed stability of this meaning to the perturbing and transformative power of a landscape undergoing comprehensive changes under the revisionary thrust of its ramifying destinations. By situating itself in the rational system of commitments, humanism posits itself as an initial condition for what already retroactively bears a minimal resemblance, if any at all, to what originally set it in motion. Sufficiently elaborated, humanism—it shall be argued—is the initial condition of inhumanism as a force that travels back from the future to alter, if not to completely discontinue, the command of its origin.

What needs to be explicated first is what it takes to make a prescription, or what one needs to do in order to count as prescribing an obligation or a duty, to link duties and revise them. But it must also be recognized that a prescription should correspond to a set of descriptions which at all times must be synchronized with the system of modern knowledge as what yields and modifies descriptions. To put it succinctly: description without prescription is the germ of resignation, and prescription without description is whim. [...]

The description of the content of human is impossible without elaborating it in the context of use and practices, while elaboration itself is impossible without following minimally prescriptive laws of commitment-making, inference, and judgment. [...] "Fraught with oughts" (Wilfrid Sellars), humanism cannot be regarded as a claim about human that can only be professed once and subsequently turned into a foundation or axiom and considered concluded. In-humanism is a nomenclature for the infeasibility of this one-time profession. [...]

1. The Picture of "Us" Drawn in Sand

The practical elaboration of making a commitment to humanity is inhumanism. If making a commitment means fully elaborating the content of such a commitment (the consequent "what else?" of what it means to be human), and if to be human means being able to enter the space of reason, then a commitment to humanity must fully elaborate how the abilities of reason functionally convert *sentience* to *sapience*.

To be human is a mark of a distinction between, on the one hand, the relation between mindedness and behavior through the intervention of discursive intentionality, and on the other hand, the relation between sentient intelligence and behavior in the absence of such mediation. It is a distinction between *sentience* as a strongly biological and natural category and *sapience* as a rational (not to be confused with logical) subject. The latter is a normative designation which is specified by entitlements and the responsibilities they bring about. It is important to note that the distinction between sapience and sentience is marked by a functional demarcation rather than a structural one. Therefore, it is still fully historical and open to naturalization, while at the same time being distinguished by its specific functional organization, its upgradable set of abilities and responsibilities, its cognitive and practical demands. The relation between sentience and sapience can be understood as a continuum that is not differentiable everywhere. While such a complex continuity might allow the naturalization of normative obligations at the level of sapience—their explanation in terms of naturalistic causes—it does not permit the extension of certain conceptual and descriptive resources specific to sapience (such as the particular level of mindedness, responsibilities, and, accordingly, normative entitlements) to sentience and beyond.

The rational demarcation lies in the difference between being capable of acknowledging a law and being solely bound by a law; between understanding and mere reliable responsiveness to stimuli. It lies in the difference between stabilized communication through concepts (as made possible by the communal space of language and symbolic forms) and chaotically unstable or transient types of response or communication (such as complex reactions triggered purely by biological states and organic requirements or group calls and alerts among social animals). Without such stabilization of communication through concepts and modes of inference involved in conception, the cultural evolution as well as the conceptual accumulation and refinement required for the evolution of knowledge as a shared enterprise would be impossible.

But insofar as reason enjoys a functional autonomy—
which enables it to prevent the collapse of sapience back
into sentience—the full elaboration of the abilities of
reason entails unpacking the consequences of the autonomy of reason for human. Humanism is by definition a
project to amplify the space of reason through elaborating what the autonomy of reason entails and what
demands it makes upon us. But the autonomy of reason
implies its autonomy to assess and construct itself, and
by extension, to renegotiate and construct that which
distinguishes itself by entering the space of reason.
In other words, the self-cultivation of reason, which is the
emblem of its functional autonomy, materializes as staggering consequences for humanity. What reason does
to itself inevitably takes effect as what it does *to* human.

Since the functional autonomy of reason implies
the self-determination of reason with regard to its own
conduct—insofar as reason cannot be assessed or revised
by anything other than itself (to avoid equivocation or
superstition)—commitment to such autonomy effectively
exposes what it means to be human to the sweeping
revisionary effect of reason. In a sense, the autonomy
of reason is the autonomy of its power to revise, and
commitment to the autonomy of reason (via the project of
humanism) is a commitment to the autonomy of reason's
revisionary program *over which human has no hold*.

Inhumanism is exactly the activation of the revisionary
program of reason against the self-portrait of humanity.
Once the structure and the function of commitment are

27

genuinely understood, we see that a commitment works its way back from the future, from the collateral commitments of one's current commitment, like a corrosive revisionary acid that rushes backward in time. By eroding the anchoring link between present commitments and their past, and by seeing present commitments from the perspective of their ramifications, revision forces the updating of present commitments in a cascading fashion that spreads globally over the entire system. The rational structure of a commitment, or more specifically, of commitment to humanity, constructs the opportunities of the present by cultivating the positive trends of the past through the revisionary forces of the future. Once you commit to human, you effectively start erasing its canonical portrait backward from the future.

It is, as Foucault suggests, the unyielding wager on the fact that the self-portrait of man will be erased, like a face drawn in sand at the edge of the sea [cit.]. Every portrait drawn is washed away by the revisionary power of reason, permitting more subtle portraits with so few canonical traits that one should ask whether it is worthwhile or useful to call what is left behind human at all.

Ultimately, the necessary content as well as the real possibility of human rests on the ability of sapience—as functionally distinct from sentience—to practice inference and approach non-canonical truth by entering the deontic game of giving and asking for reasons. It is a game solely in the sense of involving error-tolerant, rule-based practices conducted in the absence of a referee, in which taking-as-true through thinking (the mark of a believer) and making-true through acting (the mark of an agent) are constantly contrasted, gauged, and calibrated. It is a dynamic feedback loop in which the expansion of one frontier provides the other with new alternatives and opportunities for diversifying its space and pushing back its boundaries according to its own specifications.

Inhumanism is the labor of rational agency on human. But there is one caveat here: the rational agency is not personal, individual, or necessarily biological. The kernel of inhumanism is a commitment to humanity via the concurrent construction and revision of human as oriented and regulated by the autonomy of reason, i.e., its self-determination and responsibility for its own needs. In the space of reason, construction entails revision, and revision demands construction. The revision of the alleged portrait of human implies that the construction of human in whatever context can be exercised without recourse to a constitutive foundation, a fundamental identity, an immaculate nature, a given meaning, or a prior state.

---

2. A Discursive and Constructible "We"

What combines both the ability to infer and the ability to approach truth (i.e., truth in the sense of making sense of taking-as-true and making-true, separately and in conjunction with one another) is the capacity to engage discursive practices in the way that pragmatism describes it: as the ability to (1) deploy a vocabulary, (2) use a vocabulary to specify a set of abilities or practices, (3) elaborate one set of abilities-or-practices in terms of another set of abilities-or-practices, and (4) use one vocabulary to characterize another.

Discursive practices constitute the game of giving and asking for reasons and outlining the space of reason as a landscape of navigation rather than as *a priori* access to explicit norms. The capacity to engage discursive practices is what functionally distinguishes sapience from sentience. Without such a capacity, human is only a biological fact that does not by itself yield any propositional contentfulness of the kind that demands a special form of conduct and value attribution and appraisal. Without this key aspect, speaking about the history of human risks reducing the social construction to a biological supervenience while depriving history of its possibilities for intervention and reorientation.

In other words, deprived of the capacity to enter the space of reason through discursive practices, being human is barred from meaning anything in the sense of practice in relation to content. Action is reduced to meaning "just do something," collectivity can never be methodological or expressed

In short, revision is a license for further construction.

in terms of a synthesis of different abilities to envision and achieve a common task, and making commitment through linking action and understanding is untenable. We might just as well replace human with whatever we wish so as to construct a stuff-oriented philosophy and a nonhuman ethics where "to be a thing" simply warrants being good to each other, or to vegetables for that matter.*

Once discursive practices that map out the space of reason are underplayed or dispensed with, everything lapses either toward the individual or toward a noumenal alterity where a contentless plurality without any demand or duty can be effortlessly maintained. Discursive practices as rooted in language-use and tool-use generate a de-privatized but nonetheless stabilizing and contextualizing space through which true collectivizing processes are shaped. It is the space of reason that harbors the functional kernel of a genuine collectivity, a collaborative project of practical freedom referred to as "we" whose boundaries are not only negotiable but also constructible and synthetic.

One should be reminded that "we" is a mode of being, and a mode of being is not an ontological given or a domain exclusive to a set of fundamental categories or fixed descriptions. Instead, it is a conduct, a special performance that takes shape as it is made visible to others. Precluding this explicit and discursively mobilizable "we," the content of "being human" never translates to "commitment to human or to humanity." By undergirding "we," discursive practices organize commitments as ramifying trajectories between communal saying and doing, and they enact a space where the self-construction or extensive practical elaboration of humanity is a collaborative project.

Making a commitment to something means vacillating between doing something in order to count as saying it, and saying something specific in order to express and characterize that doing.

It is the movement back and forth, the feedback loop, between the two fields of claims and actions that defines sapience as distinguished from sentience. To make a commitment means "what else," "what other commitments" it brings forth and how such consequent commitments demand new modes of action and understanding, new abilities and special performances that cannot be simply substituted with old abilities because they are dictated by revised or more complex sets of demands and entitlements. Without ramifying the "what else" of a commitment by practically elaborating it, without navigating what Robert Brandom calls the rational system of commitments, a commitment has neither sufficient content nor a real possibility of assessment or development. It is as good as an empty utterance—that is, an utterance devoid of content or significance even though it earnestly aspires to be committed.

*cf. p.54

2. *When We Lost Contact with "What Is Becoming of Us"*

Whereas, as Michael Ferrer points out, antihumanism is devoted to the unfeasible task of deflating the conflation of human significance with human veneration, inhumanism is a project that begins by dissociating human significance from human glory.[cit.]

Resolving the content of conflation and extracting significance from its honorific residues, inhumanism then takes humanism to its ultimate conclusions. It does so by constructing a revisable picture of us that functionally breaks free from our expectations and historical biases regarding what this image should be, look like, or mean. For this reason, inhumanism, as it will be argued later, prompts a new phase in the systematic project of emancipation—not as a successor to other forms of emancipation but a critically urgent and indispensable addition to the growing chain of obligations.

Moreover, inhumanism disrupts a future anticipation built on descriptions and prescriptions provided by a conservative humanism. Conservative humanism places the consequentiality of human in an over-determined meaning or an over-particularized set of descriptions which is fixed and must at all times be preserved by any prescription developed by and for humans. Inhumanism, on the other hand, finds the consequentiality of commitment to humanity in its practical elaboration and in the navigation of its ramifications. For the true consequentiality of a commitment is a matter of its power to generate other commitments, to update itself in accordance with its ramifications, to open up spaces of possibility, and to navigate the revisionary and constructive imports such possibilities may contain.

The consequentiality of commitment to humanity, accordingly, lies not in how parameters of this commitment are initially described or set. Rather, it lies in how the pragmatic meaning of this commitment (its meaning through use) and the functionalist sense of its descriptions (what must we do in order to count as human?) intertwine to effectuate broad consequences that are irreconcilable with what was initially the case. It is consequentiality in the latter sense that overshadows consequentially in the former sense, before it fully proves the former's descriptive poverty and prescriptive inconsequentiality through a thoroughgoing revision.

As Robert Brandom notes, every "consequence is a change in normative status" that may lead to incompatibilities between commitments.[cit.] Therefore, in order to maintain the undertaking, we are obliged to do something specific to resolve the incompatibilities. From the perspective of inhumanism, the more discontinuous the consequences of committing to humanity, the greater are the demands of doing something to rectify our undertakings (ethical, legal, economic, political, technological, and so forth). Inhumanism highlights the urgency of action according to a tide of revision that increasingly registers itself as a discontinuity, a growing rift with no possibility of restoration.

Any sociopolitical endeavor or consequential project of change must first address this rift—or discontinuity effect—and then devise a necessary course of action in accordance with it. But doing something about the discontinuity effect—triggered by unanticipated consequences and, as a result, the exponentially growing change in normative status (that is, the demands of what ought to be done)—is not tantamount to an act of restoration. On the contrary, the task is to construct points of liaison—cognitive and practical channels— so as to enable communication between *what we think of ourselves* and *what is becoming of us*.

The ability to recognize the latter is not a given right or an inherent natural aptitude; it is, in fact, a labor, a program, that is fundamentally lacking in current political projects. Being human does not by any means entail the ability to connect with the consequences of what it means to be human. In the same vein, identifying ourselves as human is neither a sufficient condition for understanding what is becoming of us, nor a sufficient condition for recognizing what we are becoming, or more accurately, what is being born out of us.

A political endeavor aligned with antihumanism cannot forestall its descent into a grotesque form of activism. But any sociopolitical project that pledges its allegiance to conservative humanism—whether through a quasi-instrumentalist and preservationist account of reason (such as Habermasian rationality) or a theologically charged meaning of human—enforces the tyranny of here and now under the aegis of a foundational past or a root.

Antihumanism and conservative humanism represent two pathologies of history frequently appearing under the rubrics of conservation and progression—one: an account of the present that must preserve the traits of the past, and the other: an account of the present that must approach the future while remaining anchored in the past. But the catastrophe of revision erases them from the future by modifying the link between the past and the present.

3. *The Revisionary Catastrophe*

The definition of humanity according to reason is a minimalist definition whose consequences are not immediately given, but whose ramifications are staggering. If there was ever a real crisis, it would be our inability to cope with the consequences of committing to the real content of humanity. The trajectory of reason is that of a general catastrophe whose pointwise instances and stepwise courses have no observable effect or comprehensive discontinuity. Reason is therefore simultaneously a medium of stability that reinforces procedurality and a general catastrophe, a medium of radical change that administers the discontinuous identity of reason to an anticipated image of human.

Elaborating humanity according to the discursive space of reason establishes a discontinuity between human's anticipation of itself (what it expects itself to become) and the image of human modified according to its active content or significance. It is exactly this discontinuity that characterizes inhumanism as the general catastrophe ordained by activating the content of humanity, whose functional kernel is not just autonomous but also compulsive and transformative. [*continued on page 4*]

[*continues from page 4*] Rationalism as the compulsive navigation of the space of reason turns commitment to humanity into a revisionary catastrophe, by converting its initial commitment into a ramified cascade of collateral commitments which must be navigated in order for it to be counted as commitment. But it is precisely this conversion, instigated and guided by reason, that transforms a commitment into a revisionary catastrophe that travels backward in time from the future, from its revisionary ramifications, in order to interfere with the past and rewrite the present. In this sense, reason establishes a link in history hitherto unimaginable from the perspective of a present that preserves an origin or is anchored in the past.

To act in tandem with the revisionary vector of the future is not to redeem but to update and revise, to reconstitute and modify. As an activist impulse, redemption operates as a voluntaristic mode of action informed by a preservationist or conserved account of the present. Revision, on the other hand, is an obligation or a rational compulsion to conform to the revisionary waves of the future stirred by the functional autonomy of reason.

The clinical progress of kuru is remarkably uniform. It has been divided into three stages by Dr. Carleton Gajdusek, who has made extensive clinical studies of the disease:

> The first, or ambulant, stage is usually self-diagnosed before others in the community are aware that the patient is ill... Tremors are at first no different from those of slight hypersensitivity to cold; the patient shivers inordinately. Incoordination affects the lower extremities before progressing to involve the upper extremities. Patients arising to a standing posture often stamp their feet as though angry at them. In attempting to maintain balance when standing, the toes grip and claw the ground more than usual. Very early in the disease the inability to stand on one foot is a helpful diagnostic clue...

> The second, or sendentary, stage is reached when the patient can no longer walk without complete support. Tremors... become more severe and a changing rigidity of the limbs often develops, associated with widespread [repetitive muscular spasms], or sometimes shock-like muscle jerks and occasionally coarser [irregular, involuntary] movements, especially when the patient is thrown into an exaggerated startle response by postural instability, or by sudden exposure to noise or bright light... Emotional lability, leading to outbursts of pathological laughter [is] frequent, sometimes even appearing in the first stage of the disease, and smiling and laughter are terminated slowly...

> The third, or terminal, stage is reached when the patient is unable to sit up without support... Terminally, urinary and faecal incontinence develop and dysphagia [difficulty swallowing] leads to thirst and starvation... and the patient becomes mute and unresponsive.

4. *Autonomy of Reason*

But what exactly is the functional autonomy of reason? It is the expression of the self-actualizing propensity of reason—a scenario wherein reason liberates its own spaces despite what naturally appears to be necessary or happens to be the case. Here "necessary" refers to an alleged natural necessity and should be distinguished from a normative necessity. Whereas the given status of natural causes is defined by "is" (something that is purportedly the case because it has been contingently posited, such as the atmospheric condition of the planet), the normative of the rational is defined by "ought to." The former communicates a supposedly necessary impulsion while the latter is not given, but instead generated by explicitly acknowledging a law or a norm implicit in a collective practice, thereby turning it into a binding status, a conceptual compulsion, an *ought*.

It is the acknowledging, error-tolerant, revisionary dimension of ought—as opposed to the impulsive diktat of a natural law—that presents ought as a vector of construction capable of turning contingently posited natural necessities into the manipulable variables required for construction. In addition, the order of ought is capable of composing a functional organization, a chain or dynasty of oughts, that procedurally effectuates a cumulative escape from the allegedly necessary *is* crystalized in the order of here and now.

The functional autonomy of reason consists in connecting simple oughts to complex oughts or normative necessities or abilities by way of inferential links or processes. A commitment to humanity, and, consequently, the autonomy of reason, requires not only specifying what oughts or commitment-abilities we are entitled to, but also developing new functional links and inferences that connect existing oughts to new oughts or obligations. [...]

5. *Functional Autonomy*

The claim about the functional autonomy of reason is not a claim about the genetic spontaneity of reason, since reason is historical and revisable, social and rooted in practice. It is really a claim about the autonomy of discursive practices and the autonomy of inferential links between oughts, that is to say, links between constructive abilities and revisionary obligations. Reason has its roots in social construction, in communal assessment, and in the manipulability of conditionals embedded in modes of inference. It is social partly because it is deeply connected to the origin and function of language as a de-privatizing, communal, and stabilizing space of organization. But we should be careful to extract a "robust" conception of the social, because a generic appeal to social construction risks not only relativism and equivocation but also, as Paul Boghossian points out, a fear of knowledge. [cit.] The first movement in the direction of extracting this robust conception of the social is making a necessary distinction between the "implicitly" normative aspect of the social (the area of the consumption and production of norms through practices) and the dimension of the social inhabited by conventions, between norms as intervening attitudes and normalizing norms as conformist dispositions.

Reason begins with an intervening attitude toward norms implicit in social practices. It is neither separated from nature nor isolated from social construction. However, reason has irreducible needs of its own (Kant) and a constitutive self-determination (Hegel), and it can be assessed only by itself (Sellars). In fact, the first task or question of rationalism is to come up with a conception of nature and the social that allows for the autonomy of reason*. This question revolves around a causal regime of nature that allows for the autonomous performance of reason in "acknowledging" laws, whether natural or social. Therefore, it is important to note that rationality is not conduct in accordance with a law, but rather the acknowledging of a law. Rationality is the "conception of law" as a portal to the realm of revisable and navigable rules.

We only become rational agents once we acknowledge or develop a certain intervening attitude toward norms that renders them binding. We do not embrace the normative status of things outright. We do not have

---

*cf. *Nature, Its Man and His Goat (Enigmata of Natural and Cultural Chimeras)*, the author's libretto—to be read from two parallel columns of text—for *Hinge*, tracks 1 & 3 of Florian Hecker's *Articulação* (eMEGO 180), sung by Joan La Barbara and Sugata Bose & Anna Kohler, resp. (p.t.o.)

access to the explicit—that is, logically codified—status of norms. It is through such intervening attitudes toward the revision and construction of norms through social practices that we make the status of norms explicit.[cit.] Contra Hegel, rationality is not codified by explicit norms from the bottom up. To confuse implicit norms accessible through intervening practices with explicit norms is common and risks logicism or intellectualism, i.e., an account of normativity in which explicit norms constitute an initial condition with rules all the way down—a claim already debunked by Wittgenstein's regress argument.[cit.]

HINGE *
MODULATOR (... MEAN-INGLESS, AFFECTLESS, OUT OF NOTHING ...)
HINGE **

6. Functional Bootstrapping and Practical Decomposability

The autonomy of reason is a claim about the autonomy of its normative, inferential, and revisionary function in the face of the chain of causes that condition it. Ultimately, this is a (neo)functionalist claim, in the sense of a pragmatic or rationalist functionalism. Pragmatic functionalism must be distinguished from both traditional AI-functionalism, which revolves around the symbolic nature of thought, and behavioral variants of functionalism, which rely on behaviors as sets of regularities. While the latter two risk various myths of pancomputationalism (the unconditional omnipresence of computation, the idea that every physical system can implement every computation) or behavioralism, it is important to note that a complete rejection of functionalism in its pragmatic or Kantian rationalist sense will inevitably usher in vitalism and ineffabilism, the mystical dogma according to which there is something essentially special and non-constructible about thought.

Pragmatic functionalism is concerned with the pragmatic nature of human discursive practices, that is, the ability to reason, to go back and forth between saying and doing *stepwise*. Here, "*stepwise*" defines the constitution of saying and doing, claims and performances, as a condition of near-decomposability. For this reason, pragmatic functionalism focuses on the decomposability of discursive practices into nondiscursive practices. (What ought one to do in order to count as reasoning

41

or even thinking?). Unlike symbolic or classic AI, pragmatic functionalism does not decompose implicit practices into explicit—that is, logically codifiable— norms. Instead, it decomposes explicit norms into implicit practices, *knowing-that* into *knowing-how* (which is the domain of abilities endowed with boot-strapping capacities—what must be done in order to count as performing something specific?).

According to pragmatic or rationalist functionalism, the autonomy of reason implies the automation of reason, since the autonomy of practices, which is the marker of sapience, suggests the automation of discursive practices by virtue of their algorithmic decomposability into nondiscursive practices. The automation of discursive practices, or the feedback loop between saying and doing, is the veritable expression of reason's functional autonomy and the telos of the disenchantment project. If thought is able to carry out the disenchanting of nature, it is only the automation of discursive practices that is able to disenchant thought.

---

3. Intervention as Construction and Revision

Now we can turn the argument regarding the exigencies of making a commitment into an argument about the exigencies of being a human, insofar as humanism is a system of practical and cognitive commitments to the concept of humanity. The argument goes as follows: in order to commit to humanity, the content of humanity must be scrutinized. To scrutinize this content, its implicit commitments must be elaborated. But this task is impossible unless we take humanity-as-a-commitment to its ultimate conclusion—by asking what else being a human entails, by unfolding the other commitments and ramifications it brings about.

But since the content of humanity is distinguished by its capacity to engage rational norms rather than natural laws (ought instead of is), the concept of entailment for humanity-as-a-commitment is non-monotonic....

Here, automation does not imply an identical iteration of processes aimed at effective optimization or strict forms of entailment (monotonicity). It is a register of the functional analysis or practical decomposability of a set of special performances that permits the autonomous bootstrapping of one set of abilities out of another set. Accordingly, automation here amounts to practical enablement or the ability to maintain and enhance the functional autonomy or freedom. The pragmatic procedures involved in this mode of automation perpetually diversify the spaces of action and understanding insofar as the non-monotonic character of practices opens up new trajectories of practical organization and, correspondingly, expands the realm of practical freedom.

Once the game of reason as a domain of rule-based practices is set in motion, reason is able to bootstrap complex abilities out of its primitive abilities. This is nothing but the self-actualization of reason. Reason liberates its own spaces and its own demands, and in the process fundamentally revises not only what we understand as thinking, but also what we recognize as "us."

…That is to say, entailment no longer expresses a cause and its differential effect, as in physical natural laws or a deductive logical consequence. Instead, it expresses enablement and abductive non-monotonicity in the sense of a manipulable, experimental, and synthetic form of inference whose consequences are not simply dictated by premises or initial conditions.

Since non-monotonicity is an aspect of practice and complex heuristics, defining the human through practical elaboration means that the product of elaboration does not correspond with what the human anticipates or with the image it has of itself. In other words, the result of an abductive inference that synthetically manipulates parameters—the result of practice as a non-monotonic procedure—will be radically revisionary to our assumptions and expectations about what "we" is and what it entails. […]

Wherever there is functional autonomy, there is a possibility of self-actualization or self-realization as an epochal development in history. Wherever self-realization is underway, a closed positive feedback loop between freedom and intelligence, self-transformation and self-consciousness, has been established. The functional autonomy of reason is then a precursor to the self-realization of an intelligence that assembles itself, piece by piece, from the constellation of a discursively elaborative "us" qua *an open-source self*.

Rationalist functionalism, therefore, delineates a nonsymbolic—that is, philosophical—project of general intelligence in which intelligence is fully apprehended as a vector of self-realization through the maintaining and enhancing of functional autonomy. Automation of discursive practices—the pragmatic unbinding of artificial general intelligence and the triggering of new modes of collectivizing practices via linking to autonomous discursive practices—exemplifies the revisionary and constructive edge of reason as sharpened against the canonical self-portrait of human. [...]

I think about my life and I don't find myself. 'A bonding relationship with the love object'.

Once again, as Lea is talking, I think about my relationship with my children: a bonding relationship where the thought of separation never crossed my mind. Rationally, I had thought out many correct theories about their autonomy, their independence, their right to control their own lives and stand on their own feet. These had remained purely theoretical because when the time came I felt lost – a void, panic, anguish. Then questions began to occur to me: who am I? am I here? do I exist?

The other day my husband was telling the story of our married life. A fine story. I listened and at a certain point I couldn't believe what I heard: I wasn't in that story. There was only him,

REZA NEGARESTANI

8. *A Cultivating Project of Construction and Revision*

[…]Liberation is neither the initial spark of freedom nor sufficient as its content. To regard liberation as the source of freedom is an eventalist credulity that has been discredited over and over, insofar as it does not warrant the maintaining and enhancing of freedom. But to identify liberation as the sufficient content of freedom produces a far graver outcome: irrationalism, and as a result, the precipitation of various forms of tyranny and fascism.

The sufficient content of freedom can only be found in reason. One must recognize the difference between a rational norm and a natural law—between the emancipation intrinsic in the explicit acknowledgement of the binding status of complying with reason, and the slavery associated with the deprivation of such a capacity to acknowledge, which is the condition of natural impulsion. In a strict sense, freedom is not liberation from slavery. It is the continuous *unlearning* of slavery.

---

alone with his fine story. He had never seen my loneliness, my suffering, my dissatisfaction. I was struck by this and it made me think a lot. But it is true. If I think about my life up to now, I cannot put my own story together, only that of my sons. It is me for them, with them, in an intense dialogue, the three of us alone, all in one. The essence of myself transplanted in them. What about me? Why didn't I keep anything for myself? What have I done for

Ada Flaminio in *Scuola Senza Fine*, transcribed in *Off Screen: Women and Film in Italy: Seminar on Italian and American Directions* (ed. Giuliana Bruno, Maria Nadotti. Routledge Library Editions, 2016)

The compulsion to update commitments as well as construct cognitive and practical technologies for exercising such feats of commitment-updating are two necessary dimensions of this unlearning procedure. Seen from a constructive and revisionary perspective, *freedom is intelligence*. A commitment to humanity or freedom that does not practically elaborate the meaning of this dictum has already abandoned its commitment and taken humanity hostage only to trudge through history for a day or two.

Liberal freedom, be it a social enterprise or an intuitive idea of being free from normative constraints (i.e. freedom without purpose and designed action), is a freedom that does not translate into intelligence, and for this reason, it is retroactively obsolete. To reconstitute a supposed constitution, to draw a functional link between identifying what is normatively good and making it true, to maintain and enhance the good and to endow the pursuit of the better with its own autonomy—such is the course of freedom. But this is also the definition of intelligence as the self-realization of practical freedom and functional autonomy that liberates itself in spite of its constitution.

ADRIANA MONTI

Scuola Senza Fine

(Excerpt: portrait of Ada Flaminio, 1983)

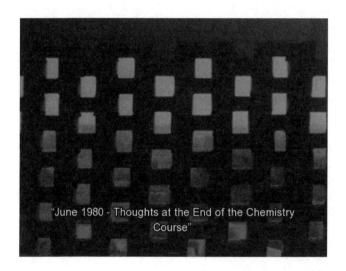

"June 1980 - Thoughts at the End of the Chemistry Course"

"The 150 Hours Courses were an educational experiment implemented in Italy beginning in 1974, available to factory workers and farmers initially, and expanding to include women a couple of years later. The courses were non-vocational; they were not intended to improve one's productivity at work, but rather to allow for personal and collective growth. The courses sought to

Doing a chemistry course made me realize that

it was the evolution of human thought that
attracted me to science.

help workers reflect not only upon their working conditions but also on their lives. A large part was devoted to the re-elaboration and reinterpretation of what was defined as the "lived experience" of those attending: their experiences with work, emigration, cultural and language discrimination, union struggles, etc. *Scuola Senza Fine* shows how the experiment extended into the lives of women

What fascinates me is that in the beginning

humans had this incredible ability to be one with nature.

taking the course, most of whom were housewives. The film was produced in collaboration with these students as part of their studies for the class, turning the curriculum's questions about the representation of women into questions about the representation of themselves. Adriana Monti writes in her introduction to the film: "After I had been working with a particular group of housewives

Later, when their thinking evolved due to their scientific discoveries,

they changed their symbols in order to represent this new objective reality.

for a year we started shooting the film *Scuola Senza Fine* (literally School Without End) almost casually, in 1979. I was able to get equipment free of charge and money to pay for the film was made available. Rediscovering the pleasure of reading and studying was reliving their adolescence. It was important for them to have teachers to whom they could tell in writing what

Today, in spite of all their scientific achievements,

modern humans still need a subjective
interpretation of love and hate,

they had done and thought, their past history and plans for the future.
The film shows how the women related to each other at that time and the
special closeness each woman felt for every other—perhaps because they
came from the same place, or shared the same ideals and way of thinking, or,
simply, because they were fond of each other. For many women, rediscovering

51

fear of life and death.

the mother/ teacher relationship meant being able to express thoughts which had often been undervalued or disregarded (most of the housewives attending the course had given up their education to go to work or had not been able to make use of the knowledge they had already, because they stayed at home after getting married). The opportunity to relive that relationship in a learning situation stimulated a very interesting kind of writing and thought." cinenova.org

KOSEN OHTSUBO

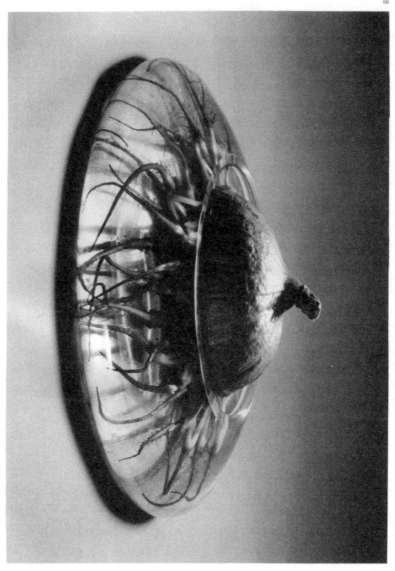

かぼちゃのくらげ　1976, 6　小松菜, かぼちゃ　15×32×32　いけ花龍生 76, 8月号

KOSEN OHTSUBO

The more serious I became, the more doubtful I became about the future of *Ikebana*... I say, I was in love with *Ikebana* that much. In other words, the way of traditional *Ikebana*'s thinking is that it is possible to define the delicate shade of the taste of leaves or branches. But don't you think there are not so many people who can feel the delicate shade of taste? Then, can those people who cannot feel it never understand *Ikebana* or art? It should not be that way. I think there should be some kind of *Ikebana* which can attract those people.

About what time did you start to deal with vegetables?
It was in the early 70s. Don't you feel that vegetables are a lump of life? And from that realistic point, they are more economical than other flower materials.

Vegetables have the reality of livelihood.
Yes. When vegetables are used in the works, there is daily life emerging. Using vegetables partly means an idea of ecology in the background. No matter how beautiful we arrange flowers, people looking at them don't ever think about the relation between human beings and plants. I think vegetables can supply more factors to think about for the viewers.

Flower Artists; Kosen Ohtsubo, Kyoto Shoin Co., 1995 ISBN 763632485 5376

* `We might just as well replace human with whatever we wish so as to construct a stuff-oriented philosophy and a nonhuman ethics where "to be a thing" simply warrants being good to each other, or to vegetables for that matter.' [p.30]

KOSEN OHTSUBO

くずれゆく植物　1975.9　青桐, キャベツ, 木箱　全長250　グループ亜土展

91

おつまみキウリ1本100円 ひなくれバーにて　1978l.6　きうり 福田繁雄創作ガラス器　33×25×25　福田繁雄と龍生 水展（銀座松屋画廊）

GERRIT NOORDZIJ

The Core of Meaning*

'HOW FAR can one remove oneself from
a knowledge of meaning,** without becoming
completely unintelligible?

It is not possible to know how far removed one is,
without knowledge of what it is, *from* which one
removes oneself.

When one knows where one comes from,
one knows where one is. If we ask "Where are
we?" As well as "Where do we want to go?",
we should also ask "Where do we come from?"

---

* Lecture recorded for TYPO Berlin, 2014 (transl. WH)
** "The credible certainty of its starting point" (cf. J.H. Prynne, p. 104)

Every thing ever made by man is "an artefact."
Q: What is the fundamental artefact, preceding all artefacts? A: The traces of a tool.

No tool is simpler than the quill, with which we can leave a simple trace, like this

or alternatively, this:

or this:

(We should take this with a pinch of salt) mathematically, these are described as *parallelograms*.

We can produce other possibilities, with this fundamental artefact: the curve.

…and we can say that the curve is built up of an infinite series of parallelograms…

…introducing the notion of stroke thickness. There is nothing more elementary than a parallelogram. Even the thinnest line is a parallelogram. A line that is no longer a parallelogram, is nothing.

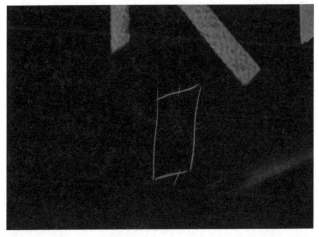

The parallelogram makes its first appearance in written records approximately 4000 years ago:

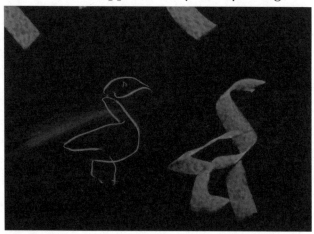

The Egyptians would *draw*—for example—a bird. And in their books of the dead they *wrote* it more efficiently with a quill (drawn hieroglyphs are not the same as written hieroglyphs).

They wrote everything in this way (with single quill-strokes). Here's a snake…

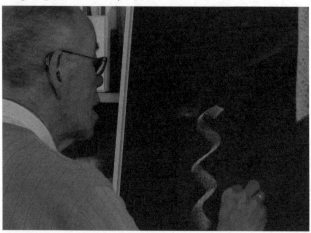

that threatens this bird and its chick:

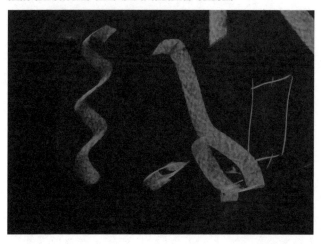

This technique was not used in the oldest known records of alphabets, where characters look like these scratched lines…

…these Egyptian records are kept on papyrus, and those Semitic, alphabetical characters are found, scratched, in clay shards.

In the Iron Age, the alphabet was copied from that of the Greeks, who had different technique:

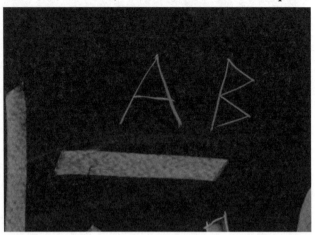

Scholars say that writing was initially logographic: an A was a sign, representing a whole word:

Writing became syllabic: the A becomes a part of a word:

Writing then becomes phonetic: the A represents a sound:

All through this, the character, A—the whole alphabet—remains the same, unchanging throughout these conditions.

"No!", say the scholars: the Greeks completed
the alphabet first, since they added the vocals.
"No!", say I: the alphabet is a set of *images*,
it doesn't contain sounds. The linguists are mis-
led, perceiving what we all normally
perceive. Yet letters that *look* like this...

or this...

or this…

…don't *contain* consonants or vocals. They
are just *capitals*, *half-uncials* and *minuscules*.
These are the proper names for the alphabet's
various shapes.

Linguists don't see what's there. One must stop
seeing and start looking. To see things for what
they are: that letters are connected to a meaning.
We shouldn't speak of writing but justification.
Meaning bridges speech and writing.

In the logographic, syllabic, and phonetic progression (of the letter A), it is assumed that
a sign cannot be *ideographic*, or directly connected to its meaning. But it can:

After dinner at a Chinese restaurant, I ask how
much the meal costs. [I don't speak Chinese, so]
I won't understand their [spoken] answer.
But they consult the price list, and next to the
[to me] incomprehensible descriptions, there
are these signs they can copy out and add up.
I definitely understood what *these* signs mean…

These signs aren't bothered by our language differences, or differences between signs and meanings. Their meaning is traced directly
onto the numbers.

Now, I believe that the alphabet was originally
a number-system. That the alphabet wasn't
developed to describe things, but simply to describe what you owe me and what I get
from you in return.

This would equate with the other legend: that
the alphabet originated on the caravan trails
of the east, where paths crossed and things were
exchanged between people who had no common
language, but did keep an administration.
These signs came in very handy.

The Greeks said the same: that *their* alphabet was
used in order to communicate with Phoenician
traders. The alphabet jumped from one culture to
another, and, to my mind, originated in numbers.
And the Romans sensibly introduced the decimal
system: ten characters are sufficient.

In the fifth century, these signs—the Latin script—
fell into the hands of Barbarians, and the development of written characters accelerated. And
all that was brought to a halt in the fifteenth
century with the invention of typesetting.

Godwit

Scattering, gathering, forming a single unit
Death/exhaustion rises up
It is the rope, koakoa [the cry of the bird]
Binding you here to me
The cry/chattering of the flock
Come close together
From inside its throat – a marauding party
A godwit
A godwit that hovers
One bird
Has settled on the sand bank
It has settled over there
It has settled over there
They have settled here

"In 1977, Hotere created […] an 18 metre long mural for Auckland International
Airport. *The Flight of the Godwit* honours the bar-tailed godwit (or kūaka),
a bird admired by Māori for its long-haul flights. Displayed in the Arrivals Hall,
the mural welcomed returning citizens and visitors alike. It exemplified many of
Hotere's key themes: the relationship between the ancient Māori worldview and
the contemporary world, and abstract art's ability to evoke questions of ecology
and cosmology. In 1996, the Airport deinstalled the mural and gifted it to the
Chartwell Trust. In 1997, Hotere restored the work, retitling it *Godwit/Kūaka*."
citygallery.org.nz

Kuaka

Ruia ruia, opea opea, tahia tahia
Kia hemo ake
Ko te kaka koakoa
Kia herea mai
Te kawai korokī
Kia tatata mai
I roto i tana pukorokoro whaikaro
He kūaka
He kūaka mārangaranga
Kotahi manu
I tau ki te tāhuna
Tau atu
Tau atu
Kua tau mai

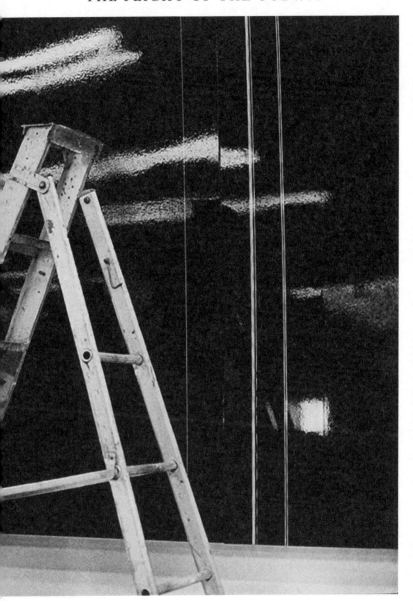

(I am) For the Birds

THEY'VE GOT THEIR OWN THING going on, birds. Whether we see them or not is irrelevant because whether they see us or not doesn't change anything. But on a park bench by a lake we are not asking each other for anything. Behaviour is not driven by looking. Neither mine nor theirs, there is no driving at all. I am looking, but I need not be. It is a trick, a trap, a game—looking, how it would have us do—because actually these birds they do not mind. They do something else instead, regardless. And so do I in fact. And this is the thing. Here we are, both doing. That is what is in this not-looking, looking away. This is what it is: an act of a special kind. Not to be looked at. A one not told. Not the usual drama. I am not figured (I am already so) and am constituted because of it. This, to co-exist, a peculiar balance on either side of the proscenium arch dividing everything.

Balanced there, birds are heard largely by chance. I am here by chance, a birdsong. He is on the balcony, a bird on a branch. It is not that one of us is there for the other, both and neither of us are pictures. Often when birds are heard they are not seen. And they do not see me. Most of the time they don't walk straight either. So it's appropriate that even when I am hearing them I am not being addressed. I am see

ing something like the drift of a catch-all frame producing
information. Peripheral, it's a relief, like the indifferent
put-put of a tennis match that I am walking past. It's
a release, a rush, no relevance. In this room we all come
and go. He does not see me and neither does anything
else. I am in a city where adverts do not make any sense.
Nothing is talking to me, nobody knows. I am not

Just so, over there the foot doesn't know and neither
does the sock. They become both each other and neither
at one and the same time, as the same form precisely,
all of me, of him. Electric. A somethingdone-to, put on,
but a nothing touched. There's the dumb thrill. In no
need. Slightly parted lips, quite far away and no hands.
Which is no more clear than when the dirty scuffs of
a clay court stay on a white sock for the whole match,
unchecked, unknown, the very mark of a not-knowing
so extreme that I am up close to it like to the concrete
corner of a swimming pool and I talk to it because it
cannot be addressed also and I tell it that it doesn't
know. Here is information, mobilised as desire, as high
drama, being ignored. It's a relief, a release, a rush.

The interference of all silence. The sound of a machine,
a scratch, dirt or its image. The radio at night. Something—work—somewhere else is being done and it does
not need to be done by me and it is being done by me.

I have left my body, I am in my body. I am not thinking, no privilege. A flag is flying and there is welding, like smoking, like somebody else smoking. Two things are happening at once. That's all. It is an equivalence that is entirely ordinary. Reorganising suspension. Here exactly at this intersection, it is the measure of me. I am thrown. Listen. Chance is heard and I am changed. Begin again

Originally written for Jimmy Robert's exhibition *Made to Measure* at 1857 gallery, Oslo, in the autumn of 2013. The text was displayed over two walls of the gallery space.

Margaret Benyon, *Bird in Box*, 1973. Laser transmission, 8" × 10".
"although officially it was a hologram of a complete closed surface,
unofficially it was about my feelings as a scapegoated female artist
in the architecture department, a boxed-in 'bird'."

psa-perloff-et-alia.tif
(Photoshop bitmap 2400dpi, Raster dot screen, -45°, 30 lpi)

* 'Marjorie' is Marjorie Perloff—to whose *Poetry on the Brink: Reinventing the Lyric*, (bostonreview.net/archives) this text responds—an authority on twentieth and twenty-first century poetry; supplier of a theoretical backbone so we might 'buff up the staturary' of the Likes of Craig Dworkin, Kenneth Goldsmith and the 'Conceptual Writing' franchise; and reproduce tags like 'unoriginality,' 'uncreative writing.'

Keston Sutherland's *Theses on Antisubjectivist Dogma* considers that 'Conceptual poets and antisubjectivists of every other poetical stripe […] are indifferent or oblivious to the history of poetic technique,' since 'there is no such thing as "traditional poetry" and there is no such thing as "the Lyric I." The use of the first person pronoun in poetry is as various and complex as the use of language itself.'

Painted Clear, Painted Black

I FEEL like the back story of Marjorie*s avant garde
mandate is mourning. I think Perloff has sustained
an enormous amount of loss in her life and along with
her championing of avant garde practice in her criticism
she's also deeply engaged in controlling the emotional
climate of the room she's in. Who gets to feel what when,
and how! And that's a problem because poetry is a
community not an institution and we're always at multiple purposes here in this room. When she opens her
piece with Jed Rasula's assertion of the problem of there
being too many poets I wonder why neither of them
notice that in the mainstream there aren't any poets.
We're mainly hearing that *no* poets are being read.
That there's no understanding of poetry today. Then
the writer, whoever cites something they used to like
or understands *as* poetry. Anything will do because
poetry has no *relevance*. The enterprise that all of us
take part in is for all intents and purposes absent in
public life today. Poetry is the absolutely denied body
of free and democratic exchange. Poetry's where men
get to feel like women always feel. Cause we're really just
not there. I agree with Marjorie that what gets rewarded
is mostly pretty damn boring. But that's because there
is *no scene*. No excess. It just doesn't get any public ink.

And this denial seems to be the empire moment. And it's why it doesn't matter to me how many poets there are. The most visible poets, the most rewarded poets are literally the ones who aren't. So in Perloff's response to Matvei's response to her original piece in *Boston Review* which was originally in *Virginia Quarterly Review* (and that's what she meant) she bothers to declare me to be a contemporary example of "transparency or feigned transparency" in poetry and I think if what she means is that my front story (unlike hers) is mourning she is absolutely right. In theory transparency used to mean that one could in some ways witness the process of the person writing. The writer was including the reader somehow. Later it referred to a kind of *aha* moment when the writer revealed an authentic self that showed all too well the workings of empire. Is that what she means that I do? In my empire of the heart. While feigning or not?

To reflect on my own writing I arrived on the scene in New York in my 20s (okay I already wrote a book about this) landing very deliberately in the avant garde where it seemed everyone I met took it upon himself to pass on to me ze avant garde canon as he saw it. There were so many approaches and rightnesses and because I already came from a doctrinaire catholic background I wasn't so open to learning from some man of my age or older "the truth." My avant garde then & now was composed of a shaky imagined grid holding a multiple of approaches. I did a magazine called *dodgems* that exemplified that.

I published Charles and I published Alice Notley and
I published Lily Tomlin. And I am always negotiating
feeling and the day. Feeling lets me know when to duck
and take space. How to edit. I think of the reader as somebody who deserves something other than a recitation
from the long phallic night of my heart whether that
recitation takes the form of personal expression or a wily
conceptual sound poem. I like an author who is aware
of reception and the body. If I think of transparency
it's the text revealing the author, it's the text responding
to the political environment, it's a distressed recording
of the history of sexual violence on women, a map of
mourning and a borrow from each thing I'm reading
that has some impact on how writing stops and starts
and what entirely it could do. There's also kind of an
ethnic class-based regional bicycle I ride, which is a
very familiar but always updating kind of speech pattern
that feels to me like home. I know "we" hate speech but
also we don't. Nobody hates speech. That's hyperbole.
When I first read Gary Snyder I saw that his pacing was
very particular and it reminded me in its way of the
bodily traces in the speech balloons of comic books and
I knew I could do something similar and I do. As a writer
one is always thrifting. The works that Perloff ultimately
loves are triumphs of that approach. Interestingly in
the theory world outside of poetry *feeling* is hot stuff.
Lots and lots of books. And it's true in the tier of
poets that Matvei cites to Marjorie that she sneers at
(academics are sort of like landlords. I'm not coming

to *your* tiny apartment today. I'm working on *this*.)
but in fact CA Conrad, Ariana Reines, Daniel Borzutsky,
Jenny Zhang, Dana Ward, Dottie Lasky, Simone White,
and Karen Weiser just to name a few are all doing un-
abashedly postmodern work that is free wheeling and
exacting in its deployment of emotion. We eventually
get there (to the emo place) in Perloff but it's a question
of the right feeling which makes me deeply uncomfortable. I think Marjorie's naming of my own transparency
has to do with sort of an easy reading of what I do and
even missing that it's multiple pronged not single so that
I don't clock you with my devices. I surround you and
use them. My work has a chameleon quality in which
it feels the room and changes. I write to hold the music
of the room. If the poet wanders in her studio and that
is the text then one can pause while the siren outside
blares or even incorporate it into the poem. One of the
most important things I know about poetry is that the
words don't need to be heard. They aren't ever. Not
all of them. And I think of that as an emotional truth.
Poems are not made out of words. They're made out
of emotional absences, rips and tears. That's the incom-
plete true fabric of the text.

At the outset of Perloff's original piece she sneers at
the "lyric speaker" (supposedly from the other team or
stream but maybe me) who "really feels the pain… of
the death of a loved one." Which just seems so macho
and destructive. In Perloff's universe one needs to access
feeling (we'll gets to this later) *in an avant garde way*.

The difficulty is that when you put it that way it's no longer aesthetics. You're talking about class. When she describes language poetry as having "provided a serious challenge to the *delicate* lyric of self-expression and direct speech…" I feel bad for the limp wristed word *delicate* because it sure takes the hit of Marjorie's contempt. In a bit she will explain for us how she traded up to conceptualism because (sigh) by the 90s language poetry "*felt* [my emphasis] compelled to be more inclusive with respect to gender, race and ethnic diversity," and then, "it became" (exasperated) "difficult to tell *what was* a language poem." With Conceptualism's arrival we have the bracing clarity of Vanessa Place's very untransparent (so Perloff says) *Statement of Facts* which appropriates accounts of sexual violence from Place's work life as a lawyer and which she uses in *Statement of Facts* to "force the reader to revaluate the meaning of seemingly simple propositions" and even begin to "wonder whether we can trust any of the 'factual' statements we are given in police reports and court testimony." And really? Is that what most of us would naturally think about here:

> Dorothy C. began crying, the man would threaten her again; at some point, he put his mouth on Dorothy C.'s breasts and neck, and asked her to put his penis in her mouth. She orally copulated him, a minute later, he turned her over and put his penis in her vagina, ejaculating outside the vagina one to five minutes later…

I think it's actually very emotionally evocative and even transparent material and yet the author and the critic's request be that we merely *evaluate* it seems like a seriously traumatized (and privileged. This hasn't happened to me!) response to these materials. And of course there's the old fashioned use of the word transparent.

I mean the traditional mode of conquest of the art or literary world by a woman of every generation is always to use her body sensationally. The naked woman will always find her way in the art world. And after all it is *her* body. Here Vanessa is showing the body she has access to which is the underclass violated body. The worthless body of the victim. I'm not suggesting it's *wrong* of her to do this. I totally get it. But it *feels* wrong somehow. And for me the biggest problem comes when Marjorie reminds us that this work is not transparent. Cause it's both awful in terms of how it feels in the room to hear these materials used that way (I feel violated) and it's transparent in the old fashioned way I began to say earlier which is that "Vanessa's *so* transparent." Sexual violence remains the highroad to success. (This work has a lotta legs.) But back to how it feels "in the room." I mean since one in three women in this country (myself included—fuck here *I* go being transparent again!) have experienced sexual violence I think many readers would have to have a wide variety of responses to these materials rather than being merely "forced to reevaluate" as one is singularly being instructed to do here. Whose courtroom in what state are we in anyhow.

"Feeling" will always interfere with the advised (and
really I mean masculine) reading of such texts but
feeling (how about we try substituting "being female"
for feeling just as a stunt) is always a problem (a good
one) in literature and feeling, and if you remember,
feeling, i.e. "feeling compelled" was language poetry's
(for Perloff) downfall. And still I want to know who or
what *was* compelling language poetry to feel that way.
The women already in the language poetry room?
New Narrative writers in the Bay Area. The fact that
people wanted grants or jobs or just realized they
looked bad. Maybe something great. That's possible.
But all of it gets compacted in Perloff's aesthetic
(whenever she has to dispense *really* swiftly with
"others" she tends to say "and so on" as if unwilling
to recite the interminable list of outsiders clamoring)
as identity politics or the politically correct. Which is
stunning language for a scholar to use. It's media speak.
It's transparent speech. Because while not self-identify-
ing one as a sexist, racist or homophobic it does offer
a way to speak over the fence to those who *know*
what you mean. But what do *you* mean? Do we know?
Among language poetry's sovereign powers Marjorie
nostalgically cites: it "demanded an end to transparency."
Meaning the refusal of the direct and indirect speech
that women and people of color and queers and assorted
weaklings of the underclasses have always employed
so they don't bump into each other, die of boredom
at work or get killed.

Later on when Marjorie discusses the work of
Peter Gizzi, Charles Bernstein, and Susan Howe she
gets to the point which is that each of them people have
undergone recent personal tragedies. And I'm feeling
wary (now because I'm about to be told about the avant
garde way of mourning. And we've already learned that
avant garde poetry might initially exclude certain people,
certain kinds of direct statements, certain *bodies* and
later by means of appropriation, pastiche all of which
everyone has been using for decades but now Marjorie
tells us that Conceptual poets are *really* using these
tools. Conceptualism I think is the first school of
poetry that has appropriated previously known tools
(like appropriation)) to tear the veils from the eyes of
(I guess) of other poets who already knew about these
things. Maybe Conceptualism is not for other poets.
Conceptualists (I mean the ones that call themselves
that) might finally and actually be making the avant
garde accessible to the masses. Because the masses
are not about reading and neither is conceptualism.
Yay.

Perloff finally holds up three very wonderful poets
(who do not claim to be conceptualists, she says)
each of them as "an example of the power of *other
people's words* to generate profound emotion…"
Which is obviously the party that language poetry
could have hung in for. It's an interesting thought.

When Charles Bernstein's poems verge on bathos
(actually they're funny and that jerky excess of "wrong
feeling" is for me how they spill over into profound feeling) Perloff claims they are actually recuperated by
means of "echo" which is what I think Peter Sloterdijk
means by "an amorous bell," a kind of deep connection
involving sound that also engages on a compassionate
level. Later Peter Gizzi's goofy (goofy good I mean) lyrics
are explained in terms that suggest they are a sort of drag.
Which would have been a great and gendered way to
describe it but why do that when Marjorie can just reach
for misogyny instead. The mythic "Echo" in Gizzi's
poems is apparently learning to "communicate in
her restricted state (O Conceptualism!) with far
more personal purpose than *her earlier gossiping…*"

The work Marjorie is describing here is important,
beautiful and profound. And appropriation has always
been the most traditional way to mourn or mark a moment.
Most people don't write. And in this writers are people
too. We use texts for all our purposes, being human.
To illustrate I think of a large reading that took place it
seemed only days after 9/11 at St. Mark's Church. There
were a wide range of approaches each poet, or performer
took when they got up to the podium. Most read somebody else's work. One woman intoned a single note
from the back of the church and walked up the center
aisle humming with it, only ceasing when she got to
the front. She faced us then in silence and it was like she
had measured the pain in the room with that one note.

It seemed obvious that the shock of what had happened
in our city was so huge that hardly anyone had *written*
a statement. But everyone could find a text to read that
they were feeling through and wanted to share. Each
one of the poets Perloff discusses is rising to an occasion
similar to what I'm describing here but in their own lives.
But I wind up feeling troubled by Marjorie's informing
us about the Pygmalion process achieved in conceptual
writing where the once womanly transparent feelings
are now successfully marshaled into order, stuffed into
the echoaic format. The difficulty of reading Perloff's
criticism is that the work she's touting is held aloft like
these are the poster children for better suffering while
Rita Dove's sad marionettes are stupid, the poets in
that book *think* they are experiencing suffering, bah!
Perloff's dismissiveness feels way other than entirely
formal which becomes the problem with her entire
argument. Language poetry didn't lose its shit in the
90s because the S police were banging down the door.
Feeling is an inside and outside gong. It's history.
But Perloff's busily backing someone out of the lot,
rolling in the next ones, shit happens she shrugs, and
as informed readers we're supposed to go uh huh
and get on with helping her buff up the new statuary.
The need for feeling in poetry is of utmost importance
to Perloff, but what I come away with is that it's the
quality of the feelers (meaning whose) that's the thing
most important and true. Which is very postmodern,
incredibly elitist and certainly transparent to boot.

Un Jardin d'Hiver

Bruxelles

1974

PALACE SCRIPT
SERIES 427

14 point* — 5 lbs. A 6 a 40
The Art of Fine Printing is to Arrange Type so as to produce
a Graceful and Orderly Page that puts no Strain on the Eye

18 point* — 5 lbs. A 4 a 20
The Art of Fine Printing is to Arrange Type
so as to Produce a Graceful and Orderly Page

24 point* — 5 lbs. A 3 a 12
The Art of Fine Printing is to Set
Type so as to Produce a Graceful and

30 point* — 10 lbs. A 3 a 15
The Art of Fine Printing is to
Arrange Type so as to Produce a

36 point* — 10 lbs. A 3 a 12
The Art of Fine Printing
is to Arrange Type so as to

42 point — 10 lbs. A 2 a 5
The Art of Printing

Founts include Suitable Spaces and are Sold at a Special Rate

ABCDEFGHIJKLMNOPQRS
TUVWXYZ & Lt 1234567890 / £ $ a œ
abcdefghijklmnopqrsßtuvwxyæ .,:;?'!()

Mc Mc Mc
These extra characters are available in 14, 18 and 24 point only

153

4

92

UNIVERS BOLD CONDENSED
SERIES 694

6D on 7 point   5 lbs. A 75 a 150
THE ART OF FINE PRINTING IS TO ARRANGE TYPE so as to produce a graceful and orderly page that

7D on 8 point   5 lbs. A 70 a 140
THE ART OF FINE PRINTING IS TO ARRANGE type so as to produce a graceful and orderly

8D on 9 point   5 lbs. A 60 a 120
THE ART OF FINE PRINTING IS TO arrange type so as to produce a graceful and

9D on 10 point   10 lbs. A 90 a 180
THE ART OF FINE PRINTING IS TO set type so as to produce a graceful

10D on 11 point   10 lbs. A 80 a 130
THE ART OF FINE PRINTING IS to arrange type so as to produce

11D on 12 point   10 lbs. A 60 a 120
THE ART OF FINE PRINTING is to arrange type so as to

12D on 13 or 14 point   10 lbs. A 50 a 100
THE ART OF FINE PRINTING is to arrange type so as

14D on 16 point   10 lbs. A 35 a 65
THE ART OF FINE printing is to arrange type

18D on 20 or 24 point   10 lbs. A 20 a 40
THE ART OF FINE printing is to set

22D on 24 point   10 lbs. A 14 a 22
THE ART OF fine printing is

28D on 30 point   10 lbs. A 8 a 16
THE ART of fine printing

36 point   10 lbs. A 5 a 11
THE ART of finest

48 point   20 lbs. A 6 a 12
The Finer Arts

ABCDEFGHIJKLMNOPQRSTUVWXYZ&£1234567890
abcdefghijklmnopqrstuvwxyz., ''::-?!()

180

5

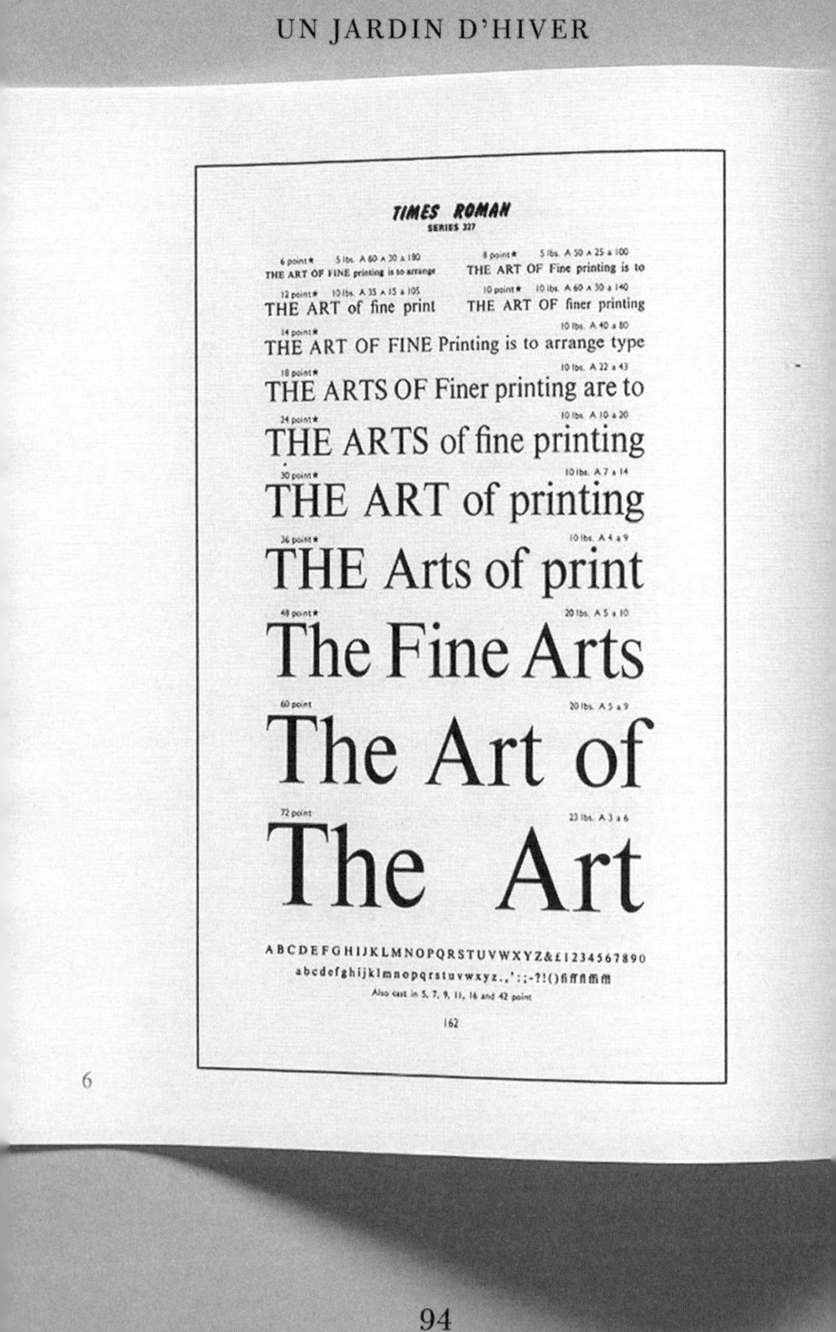

UN JARDIN D'HIVER

TIMES ROMAN
SERIES 327

6 point★ 5 lbs. A 60 a 30 a 180	8 point★ 5 lbs. A 50 a 25 a 100
THE ART OF FINE printing is to arrange	THE ART OF Fine printing is to
12 point★ 10 lbs. A 35 a 15 a 105	10 point★ 10 lbs. A 60 a 30 a 140
THE ART of fine print	THE ART OF finer printing

14 point★ 10 lbs. A 40 a 80
THE ART OF FINE Printing is to arrange type

18 point★ 10 lbs. A 22 a 43
THE ARTS OF Finer printing are to

24 point★ 10 lbs. A 10 a 20
THE ARTS of fine printing

30 point★ 10 lbs. A 7 a 14
THE ART of printing

36 point★ 10 lbs. A 4 a 9
THE Arts of print

48 point★ 20 lbs. A 5 a 10
The Fine Arts

60 point 20 lbs. A 5 a 9
The Art of

72 point 23 lbs. A 3 a 6
The Art

ABCDEFGHIJKLMNOPQRSTUVWXYZ&£1234567890
abcdefghijklmnopqrstuvwxyz.,':;-?!()fiffflffiffl
Also cast in 5, 7, 9, 11, 16 and 42 point

162

6

PERPETUA BOLD ITALIC
SERIES 461 It.

24 point   10 lbs. A 12 a 24

THE ART OF FINE PRINT
is to arrange type so as to

30 point   10 lbs. A 6 a 12

THE ARTS OF FINER
Printing are to Arrange

36 point   10 lbs. A 4 a 8

THE ART OF FINE
Printing is to Set

42 point   20 lbs. A 7 a 15

THE ARTS OF
Finer Print are

48 point   20 lbs. A 6 a 12

THE ART OF
Fine Printing

123

7

UNIVERS BOLD CONDENSED
SERIES 694

6D on 7 point
THE ART OF FINE PRINTING IS TO ARRANGE TYPE so as to produce a graceful and orderly page that
5 lbs. A 75 a 150

7D on 8 point
THE ART OF FINE PRINTING IS TO ARRANGE type so as to produce a graceful and orderly
5 lbs. A 70 a 140

8D on 9 point
THE ART OF FINE PRINTING IS TO arrange type so as to produce a graceful and
5 lbs. A 60 a 120

9D on 10 point
THE ART OF FINE PRINTING IS TO set type so as to produce a graceful
10 lbs. A 90 a 180

10D on 11 point
THE ART OF FINE PRINTING IS to arrange type so as to produce
10 lbs. A 80 a 130

11D on 12 point
THE ART OF FINE PRINTING is to arrange type so as to
10 lbs. A 60 a 120

12D on 13 or 14 point
THE ART OF FINE PRINTING is to arrange type so as
10 lbs. A 50 a 100

14D on 16 point
THE ART OF FINE printing is to arrange type
10 lbs. A 35 a 65

18D on 20 or 24 point
THE ART OF FINE printing is to set
10 lbs. A 20 a 40

22D on 24 point
THE ART OF fine printing is
10 lbs. A 14 a 27

28D on 30 point
THE ART of fine printing
10 lbs. A 6 a 16

36 point
THE ART of finest
10 lbs. A 5 a 11

48 point
The Finer Arts
20 lbs. A 6 a 12

ABCDEFGHIJKLMNOPQRSTUVWXYZ&£1234567890
abcdefghijklmnopqrstuvwxyz.,'';:-?!()

180

A WINTER GARDEN

120 copies of this opuscule by Marcel Broodthaers have been printed. It has been edited jointly by the Petersburg Press London and the Société des Expositions Brussels.

The author and I are of the opinion that it could serve as a commentary on the setting entitled 'A Winter Garden' which was mounted at the Palais des Beaux-Arts Brussels in January 1974.

Yves Gevaert

M. B. 95/120

28

Marcel Broodthaers, *Un jardin d'Hiver (A winter garden)*
London/Brussels: Société des Expositions/The Petersburg Press, 1974
28 pp., 20 × 20 cm., softcover. Edition of 120 initialed and numbered copies

Dear Charles Olson,

Very many thanks for yours*, which
was strangely exciting to have down
here in the depths of the museum. I have
written off to Robert Duncan to ask for
his IDEAS, which sounds full of interest;
but I doubt I could hope to print it. You
can have no idea how hostile the parochial
mediocrity of an English university can
be—hence I intend giving the wiseacres no
foothold in prose theory. I would rather
work to a private circulation & print what
needs to come out (like ORIGIN), but don't
have the choice as things are. So my main
hopes are for high and various quality in
the verse itself, where readers will have
to earn their insights.

[I] saw your GRAMMAR—a "book." My
concerns are very close to yours here,
but perhaps at a slight angle: thus I am
launched into the derivation problem,
and hope you will bear with it. **

---

* Responding to Olson's first letter, this is the third letter in what became a
nine-year correspondence, reproduced in *The collected letters of Charles Olson
and J. H. Prynne* (ed. Ryan Dobran. University of New Mexico Press, 2017).
** Ditto.

I am struck with the need to readjust
parts of THE CHINESE WRITTEN CHARACTER,
as a chap-book, towards some sense of the
hinges in European language or its northern groupings considered in general. "The
transference of force from agent to object,"
writes Fenollosa, "which constitute natural phenomena, occupy time. Therefore,
a reproduction of them in imagination
requires the same temporal order." Here
[Pound] interposes the gloss, "Style, that
is to say limpidity, as opposed to rhetoric."[1]
Hence the simple declarative sentence with
one transitive & active verb, furnishes
the kinetic type. But where are the sources
of this force, how is access to them won
out of the ambient silences which surround
the man on the brink of speech? From the
things themselves has been the answer,
and in the final reckoning always must be.

---

1. Ernest Fenollosa and Ezra Pound, "The Chinese Written Character as a
Medium for Poetry"*** (1919), in Ezra Pound's *Poetry and Prose: Contributions
to Periodicals*, III, 491. The first phrase should read: "The transferences
of force from agent to agent."   (like)
                                    ***
'sun' (日) + 'tree' (木) = 'East' (東) /
sun tangled in tree's branches, suggesting a sunrise (in the East)

"The Chinese pictogram as prototype"	(for)
"The Ideogrammatic Method"	(as)
"the role of the individual word in creating images"	(, so)
"allowing poetry to deal with abstract content	
through concrete images."	(Hence)
"his predilection for sentences with a transitive verb,	
which signals action, and his aversion to the stasis	
of grammar, logic and the copula"	
	(, in this,)
"a study of the fundamentals of all aesthetics."	

Things are nouns, and particular substan-
tives of this order are storehouses of
potential energy, hoard up the world's
available motions. But there are other energies: the compelling human necessities, the
exhaling of breath, the sugar which feeds the
muscles of the diaphragm & lung. It seems
probable that this source was channeled into
speech simultaneously with if not before,
the substantive pictogram or derived lexi-
graph. To sing is to modulate and make audi-
ble the breathing, declare the body's func-
tioning, its various rhythms, like shouting
or the groan of agony. Phonetic and imagis-
tic unit in this way may have evolved side by
side, as Doblhofer suggests: "Until quite
recently it was believed that all writing
without exception originated from a pictori-
al representation of concepts subsequently
evolving, as was the case in the East, ' from
the image to the letter. ' Today we are
inclined to believe that the letter existed
from the very outset and that the principal
creators of 'Western' writings (Anatolian,
Alpine and possibly Old Iberian) had already
discovered the isolated sound by the time
the Greeks adopted and adapted the Phoenician alphabet, bringing about a reciprocal
fusion and fecundation of the image and the
letter. " (Zeichen und Wunder)[2]

Even Chinese is not as exclusively visual an idiom as one might have assumed from
THE CHARACTER; phonetic compounds appear
very early, and are very extensive. Thus
the name of a tree might be borrowed to
make up a new compound, shedding its tree
determinative, just for its sound ([pi] for
example). Complex abstract notions are,
it seems, commonly formed in this way, on
the basis of transferred or borrowed sound
values. Similarly unvisual are the ' cenematic' elements in the Chinese vocabulary,
less numerous but much more common than
the ' plerematic' elements. These function
not as representational signs but as grammatical, syntactical, modal structuring
agents; number, gender, case, person,
tense, mood are cenematic functions, as
are conjunctions, correlatives, causal,
temporal, conditional, interrogative and
other such constructions. Only the plerematic words (though the categories over-
lap) function primarily as content- words,
and it is these that THE CHARACTER most
considers—the substantive furnishings
of the universe, the nouns among which
and the verbs along whose lines we live.

2. Ernst Doblhofer, Zeichen und Wunder: die Entzifferung verschollener
Schriften und Sprachen (Berlin: Paul Ne , 1957). Prynne's translation.
1961 17

But a language must accommodate both these
aspects ('locative' & 'instrumental,'
perhaps), and as [W.A.C.H.] Dobson points
out, Chinese is no exception: "In a language in which the pitch and contour of
words is part of their intrinsic phonetic
shape, pitch and contour ('intonation')
if used as an emphatic or modal device,
cannot be imposed on the word itself,
but is, as in the case, imposed upon a
class of morpheme in its environment,
existing specifically for that purpose."[3]
Thus it makes a difference to write

   WINDS   :   BENDING TREES

rather than
   THE WINDS ==> BEND ==> THE TREES

but we are still in Fenollosa's world with
either version. But the human agent, once
on the scene, immediately introduces his
own impalpable forces. I BREAK THE TREE
depends for its kinematics on our belief
in the 'I' as a source of the necessary
energies, in the pitch and contour of his
actions. The agent must be grounded in
some credible forcefulness, so fixed down
and planted that his exertions can have

---

3. W.A.C.H. Dobson, Late Archaic Chinese; a Grammatical Study, University of
Toronto Press, 1959.

direction outward and away from himself.
In a more fluid medium, for example drift-
ing through sea-water, the human agent may
take his choice between

   I BUMPED A PIECE OF DRIFTWOOD

or
   I WAS BUMPED BY A PIECE OF DRIFTWOOD

or simply
   CONTACT OCCURRED BETWEEN ME AND A PIECE
   OF DRIFTWOOD.

What makes the difference then, so articu-
lates the sentence that it may move with
purpose & effect along its own line,
outward from the agent, the object,
the lungs? Its continued momentum, it
seems to me, past and round and athwart
changes in course and direction, and the
credible certainty of its starting point.
The two depend inseparably one upon the
other. The movement founds the origin
and the origin impels the movement:
equal and opposite reaction perhaps.
And if it needs no question how the rocks
on the shore may allow us to push on them
to start out to sea, how is the human agent

so endowed, with the right to function as
the noun (pro- noun) subject of the sentence (his own life)? Commonly of course
humanity is not so endowed, lives on the
most fragile of credit, on a purely virtu-
al instrument devised and maintained by
the tacit agreement of others never to ask
to see the map for themselves. Access to
the fundament is earned by the mind's
geologers, the passions which will forge
out availably valid starting points and
lend them to those few others prepared to
profit. Writers have always done this, and
poets have always gone deeper & more tena-
ciously than any into these soundless
risks. What is brought to the encounter
is patience and restraint and a developed
sense of personal dimension, the casual-
ness of a respect rooted in desperation.
What is finally earned is place—the object
—the first noun with its own weight.
It is [Martin] Heidegger who sees this
most clearly, being the one philosopher
to recognise his dependency on the poet
(in this case [Friedrich] Holderlin),
and the insights buried in etymology.
["Everything that, by way of conception
and statement, might interpose itself
between us and thing must, first of all,

be set aside. Only then do we allow ourselves the undistorted presence of the
thing. But this allowing ourselves an
immediate encounter with the thing is
something we do not need either to demand
or to arrange. It happens slowly."][4]
And by an inverse law his shapes will
make their own way, for sure, out from
this achieved centre.

Once the noun is won and the right to
the pro-noun earned, the simple declarative
sentence becomes kinetically feasible.
Not simply the locative gesture, SEE OVER
THERE A TREE, but all the implicit passion
of I SEE A TREE or even I DO SEE THIS TREE,
NOW, FROM WHERE I AM STANDING; the poet has
won his first melody, is singing. The tree
has entered his voice, because he knows,
with terrible certainty, where he stands.
He has founded a race of pronouns, and
these bring in the potential accuracies of
adverb and adjective in regulation of this
commerce, the passage of vital airs over
his teeth & tongue & lips. Here are his
certainties, and thus far little difficulty and perhaps little argument. But whence
his confidence, whence his consciousness

---

4. Martin Heidegger, "The Origin of the Work of Art," in *Off the Beaten Track*,
p.7. (Prynne transcribed the German original).

of such certainty–how can he not merely use
his nouns in speaking, but know they are
there when he is silent? One of the most
far- ranging answers seems to lie (at least
for European, or for English) in correla-
tion, the syntax of articulated dependency. I SEE THE TREE WHICH YOU TOLD ME OF:
a new dimension has appeared by virtue
of the right- angled bend about WHICH.
Where does it take its pivotal certainty
from, its fixity as a landmark by which to
alter course? From the fundament of I and
TREE. In the earlier Germanic tongues the
leaning dependency of such syntax was much
more stressed: I SEE THAT TREE, WHICH YOU
TOLD ME OF, so that the turn was buttressed
from both sides. Thus in the Anglo Saxon
Chronicle (entry for 755 A. D.) we find
"Ðā on morgenne gehīerdun þæt þæs cyninges
þegnas þe him beæ an wærun, þæt se cyning
ofslǣgen wæs; þā ridon hīe þider…" (When
in the morning they heard that thing,
those thanes of the king who were [i. e. ,
had been left] behind him, that the king
had been killed; then they rose thither…).
Such constructions, even as densely
interknit as this, were very frequent, as
if every change in direction or introduced
dependency had to be firmly rooted in an

unambiguously demonstrative antecedent:
place must exist before departure. In German the correlative construction for THE
TIME... WHEN is still DIE ZEIT... WO (The time
where). From here follows a whole range of
clausal possibilities: for this reason....
that; with this proviso... that; despite
this fact... that; in order... that; so... that;
and so on. (Consider the way a new nomina-
tive subject is introduced in the following: "Ðā cōmon for forðy onweg ðe ðāra ōþerra
scipu āsæton."–"They got for this reason
away, that there the others' ships went
aground.")[5] Thus a reliable fundament
(noun & pro-noun): roughly physical world
and human body establishes innumerable
pivots, and it is by the act of leverage
upon these pivots that we feel their secu-
rity and our motion. The sentence swings
around its BECAUSE and ALTHOUGH and THAT
(our native cenematics), and the inertial
force which such a change of direction
generates will confirm and corroborate the
fundament while still depending upon it.
Clauses joined in apposition across commas
accumulate similar pressures: passion
speaks out in the turns and joins, which
regulate and so define the concern by the

---

5. Entry for AD 896.

rhythms thus generated. (The bending of
aluminum, say, as Against Wisdom &c.)[6] [...]

The sense of turn it is (I find) which
generates its characteristically intense
node of excitement, makes the construction
of any sentence an absorbing venture.
(It will have become evident by now that
I cannot accept Sapir's hypothesis which
you cite in your IVth section "ordering."[7]
He would have a much harder job with conjunctions.) And throughout, the gravity of
these induced concerns, this felt linkage,
depends always upon the centre, which will
be the substance of the originative nouns,
the firm personal presence of the pronouns. The whole outward thrust into
abstract utterance and totally non- refer-
ential syntax reaches back into the personal quadrant of now intersecting with
here & giving definition to both FROM and
TO (the prepositions which shape our
lives). Sentences like HE WOULD PREFER
NOT TO HAVE COME UNTIL AFTER YESTERDAY
live on the efforts of other sentences;
but it also may live through the breath

---

6. See Olson, "Against Wisdom as Such" (1954), in Collected Prose, 263.
7. See Olson, "GRAMMAR—a 'Book,'" section IV, entitled "Syntax ('ordering')," which o ers three quotations from Edward Sapir, Language: An
Introduction to the Study of Speech (New York: Harcourt Brace Jovanovich,
1949), 113–14.

across the teeth, and here again the fundament lies in the diaphragm, the speaking body, his last meal & his enduring concerns. In short, it has the occasion, and may live from this. Already in Shakespeare's time this was consciously known, and is the foundation of Ben Jonson's English Grammar: "All the parts of Syntaxe have already been declared. There resteth one general Affection of the whole, dispersed thorow every member thereof, as the bloud is thorow the body; and consisteth in the breathing, when we pronounce any Sentence; For, whereas our breath is by nature so short, that we cannot continue without a stay to speake long together; it was thought necessarie, as well as for the speakers ease, as for the plainer deliverance of the things spoken, to invent this meanes, whereby men pausing a pretty while, the whole speech might never the worse be understood" (Of the Distinction of Sentences).[8] Thus access to the pressure of solid bedrock & a fixed personal quadrant lies below and behind and at the root of every outward gesture: to comprehend HERE without shouting about it is to sing over the farthest horizon.

---

8. Ben Jonson, The English Grammar [c. 1619] (London, 1640), chapter IX, 83.

J.H.PRYNNE

Thus anyway a sketch of how I have felt
for some time about these problems, the
energies that derivation may found and
release. Your cosmogonic proem to MAXIMUS,
FROM DOGTOWN-I tells me how you stand
here, and demonstrates the matching concerns to those which started off the PRO-
JECTIVE VERSE PIECE. "the man awake lights
up from the sleeping"-kindles indeed into
various passions, outward from the earth
of which his body is made.[9] I need hardly
say how excited and moved I am by this
piece. I hope you will find something for
PROSPECT, and perhaps find time to give
me some of your reactions to it all, tell
me if I run on too long. And I'll send
a copy of PROSPECT #5 which has a piece
of mine (dressed in impeccable academic
prose, to keep the vultures out) about
some closely related issues.[10] Meanwhile,
I have followed up your leads, & am grateful for them.

Best wishes, J. H. Prynne

---

9. Maximus II, 2.
10. Prynne refers to his brief essay "Resistance and Diffculty."

P. 22

Old people in the South Fore, whose memory of the matter appears unclouded, describe their attraction to human flesh. There was no thought of acquiring the power or personality of the deceased. Nor is it correct to speak of ritual cannibalism, although many medical and journalistic accounts do so... Fore attitudes toward the bodies they consumed revolved around their fertilizing, rather than their moral, effect. Dead bodies buried in gardens encouraged the growth of crops. In a similar manner human flesh, like pig meat, helps some humans regenerate.

P. 53 – 54

In the mid-1950s, the North Fore met Ronald and Catherine Berndt with the friendly greeting, "I eat you," an apt metaphor of incorporation for the endocannibal, where food equals substance equals kinship. Since the very idea of a social relationship rests on the sharing and exchange of food, ambiguity in social relations leads to the concern that shared or exchanged food may be polluted or poisoned... The rejection of food is a denial of kinship.

P. 178

Fore myths depict an original being (bagina) creating the land as well as the guardian spirits (amani), whose descendants make up the clans found on the land today. Just as the bagina created the founding amani, it was the duty of humans to ensure that the dead were transformed into living ancestors. By eating the dead, the female affines of the deceased person confined the dangerous ghost inside themselves, thus protecting the family from ghostly attack and the pollution from a decomposing body. The final mortuary ritual enabled the ghost to depart to the land of the ancestors, the deceased person finally being reborn as an ancestor.

Vaster than Empires and More Slow

YOU'RE LOOKING AT A CLOCK. It has hands, and figures arranged in a circle. The hands move. You can't tell if they move at the same rate, or if one moves faster than the other. What does *than* mean? There is a relationship between the hands and the circle of figures, and the name of this relationship is on the tip of your tongue; the hands are ... something-or-other, at the figures. Or is it the figures that ... at the hands? What does *at* mean? They are figures—your vocabulary hasn't shrunk at all—and of course you can count, one two three four etc., but the trouble is you can't tell which one is one. Each one is one: itself. Where do you begin? Each one being one, there is no, what's the word, I had it just now, something-ship, between the ones. There is no between. There is only here and here, one and one. There is no there. Maya has fallen. All is here now one. But if all is now and all here and one all, there is no end. It did not begin so it cannot end. Oh God, here now One get me out of this—

I'm trying to describe the sensations of the average person in NAFAL flight. It can be much worse than this for some, whose time-sense is acute. For others it is restful, like a drug-haze freeing the mind from the tyranny of hours. And for a few the experience is certainly mystical;

the collapse of time and relation leading them directly to intuition of the eternal. But the mystic is a rare bird, and the nearest most people get to God in paradoxical time is by inarticulate and anguished prayer for release.

They used to drug people for the long jumps, but stopped the practice when they realized its effects. What happens to a drugged, or ill, or wounded person during near-lightspeed flight is, of course, indeterminable. A jump of ten lightyears should logically make no difference to a victim of measles or gunshot. The body ages only a few minutes; why is the measles patient carried out of the ship a leper, and the wounded man a corpse? Nobody knows, except perhaps the body, which keeps the logic of the flesh, and knows it has lain festering, bleeding, or drugged into mindlessness, for ten years. Many imbeciles having been produced, the Fisher King Effect was established as fact, and they stopped using drugs and transporting the ill, the damaged, and the pregnant. You have to be in common health to go NAFAL, and you have to take it straight.

But you don't have to be sane.

It was only during the earliest decades of the League that Earthmen, perhaps trying to bolster their battered collective ego, sent out ships on enormously long voyages, beyond the pale, over the stars and far away. They were seeking for worlds that had not, like all the known worlds, been settled or seeded by the Founders on Hain, truly alien worlds; and all the crews of these Extreme Surveys were of unsound mind. Who else would go out to collect information that wouldn't be received for four, or five, or six centuries? Received by whom? This was before the invention of the instantaneous communicator; they would be isolated both in space and time. No sane person who has experienced time-slippage of even a few decades between near worlds would volunteer for a round trip of a half millennium. The Surveyors were escapists; misfits; nuts.

Ten of them climbed aboard the ferry at Smeming Port on Pesm, and made varyingly inept attempts to get to know one another during the three days the ferry took getting to their ship, *Gum*. Gum is a Low Cetian nickname, on the order of Baby or Pet. There was one Low Cetian on the team, one Hairy Cetian, two Hainishmen, one Beldene, and five Terrans; the ship was Cetian-built, but chartered by the Government of Earth. Her motley crew came aboard wriggling through the coupling-tube one by one like apprehensive spermatozoa fertilizing the universe. She flittered for the navigator put *Gum* underway. She zittered for some hours on the edge of space a few hundred million miles from Pesm, and then abruptly vanished.

When, after ten hours twenty-nine minutes, or 256 years, *Gum* reappeared in normal space, she was supposed to be in the vicinity of Star KG-E-9665 1. Sure enough, there was the cheerful gold pinhead of the star. Somewhere within a four-hundred-million-kilometer sphere there was also a greenish planet, World 4470, as charted by a Certain Mapmaker long ago. The ship now had to find the planet. This was not quite so easy as it might sound, given a four hundred-million-kilometer haystack. And *Gum* couldn't bat about in planetary space at near lightspeed; if she did, she and Star K G – E – 9665 1 and World 4470 might all end up going bang. She had to creep, using rocket propulsion, at a few hundred thousand miles an hour. The Mathematician/ Navigator, Asnanifoil, knew pretty well where the planet ought to be, and thought they might raise it within ten E - days. Meanwhile the members of the Survey team got to know one another still better.

"I can't stand him," said Porlock, the Hard Scientist (chemistry, plus physics, astronomy, geology, etc.), and little blobs of spittle appeared on his moustache. "The man is insane. I can't imagine why he was passed as fit to join a Survey team, unless this is a deliberate experiment in non-compatibility, planned by the Authority, with us as guinea pigs."

"We generally use hamsters and Hainish gholes," said Mannon, the Soft Scientist (psychology, plus psychiatry, anthropology, ecology, etc.), politely; he was one of the Hainishmen. "Instead of guinea pigs. Well, you know, Mr. Osden is really a very rare case. In fact, he's the first fully cured case of Render's Syndrome—a variety of infantile autism which was thought to be incurable. The great Terran analyst Hammergeld reasoned that the cause of the autistic condition in this case is a super-normal emphatic capacity, and developed an appropriate treatment. Mr. Osden is the first patient to undergo that treatment, in fact he lived with Dr. Hammergeld until he was eighteen. The therapy was completely successful."

"Successful?"

"Why, yes. He certainly is not autistic."

"No, he's intolerable!"

"Well, you see," said Mannon, gazing mildly at the saliva-flecks on Porlock's mustache, "the normal defen- sive-aggressive reaction between strangers meeting—let's say you and Mr. Osden just for example— is something you're scarcely aware of; habit, manners, inattention get you past it; you've learned to ignore it, to the point where you might even deny it exists. However, Mr. Osden, being an empath, feels it. Feels his feelings, and yours, and is hard put to say which is which. Let's say that there's a normal element of hostility towards any stranger in your emotional reaction to him when you meet him, plus a spontaneous dislike of his looks, or clothes, or handshake—it doesn't matter what. He feels that dislike. As his autistic defense has been unlearned, he resorts to an aggressive defense mechanism, a response in kind to the aggression which you have unwittingly projected onto him." Mannon went on for quite a long time.

"Nothing gives a man the right to be such a bastard," Porlock said.

"He can't tune us out?" asked Harfex, the Biologist, another Hainishman.

"It's like hearing," said Olleroo, Assistant Hard Scientist, stooping over to paint her toenails with fluorescent lacquer. "No eyelids on your ears. No Off switch on empathy. He hears our feelings whether he wants to or not."

"Does he know what we're *thinking*?" asked Eskwana, the Engineer, looking round at the others in real dread.

"No," Porlock snapped. "Empathy's not telepathy! Nobody's got telepathy."

"Yes," said Mannon, with his little smile. "Just before I left Hain there was a most interesting report in from one of the recently rediscovered worlds, a hilfer named Rocannon reporting what appears to be a teachable telepathic technique existent among a mutated hominid race; I only saw a synopsis in the HILF *Bulletin*, but—" He went on. The others had learned that they could talk while Mannon went on talking; he did not seem to mind, nor even to miss much of what they said.

"Then why does he hate us?" Eskwana asked. "Nobody hates you, Ander honey," said Olleroo, daubing Eskwana's left thumbnail with fluorescent pink. The engineer flushed and smiled vaguely.

"He acts as if he hated us," said Haito, the Coordinator. She was a delicate-looking woman of pure Asian descent, with a surprising voice, husky, deep, and soft, like a young bullfrog. "Why, if he suffers from our hostility, does he increase it by constant attacks and insults? I can't say I think much of Dr. Hammergeld's cure, really, Mannon; autism might be preferable..."

She stopped. Osden had come into the main cabin. He looked flayed. His skin was unnaturally white and thin, showing the channels of his blood like a faded roadmap in red and blue. His Adam's apple, the muscles that circled his mouth, the bones and ligaments of his wrists and hands, all stood out distinctly as if displayed for an anatomy lesson. His hair was pale rust, like long-dried blood. He had eyebrows and lashes, but they were visible only in certain lights; what one saw was the bones of the eyesockets, the veining of the lids, and the colorless eyes. They were not red eyes, for he was not really an albino, but they were not blue or gray; colors had canceled out in Osden's eyes, leaving a cold waterlike clarity, infinitely penetrable. He never looked directly at one. His face lacked expression, like an anatomical drawing, or a skinned face.

"I agree," he said in a high, harsh tenor, "that even autistic withdrawal might be preferable to the smog of cheap secondhand emotions with which you people surround me. What are you sweating hate for now, Porlock? Can't stand the sight of me? Go practice some auto-eroticism the way you were doing last night, it improves your vibes. —Who the devil moved my tapes, here? Don't touch my things, any of you. I won't have it."

"Osden," said Asnanifoil, the Hairy Cetian, in his large slow voice, "why *are* you such a bastard?"

Ander Eskwana cowered down and put his hands in front of his face. Contention frightened him. Olleroo looked up with a vacant yet eager expression, the eternal spectator.

"Why shouldn't I be?" said Osden. He was not

looking at Asnanifoil, and was keeping physically as far away from all of them as he could in the crowded cabin. "None of you constitute, in yourselves, any reason for my changing my behavior."

Asnanifoil shrugged; Cetians are seldom willing to state the obvious. Harfex, a reserved and patient man, said, "The reason is that we shall be spending several years together. Life will be better for all of us if—"

"Can't you understand that I don't give a damn for all of you?" Osden said, took up his microtapes, and went out. Eskwana had suddenly gone to sleep. Asnanifoil was drawing slipstreams in the air with his finger and muttering the Ritual Primes. "You cannot explain his presence on the team except as a plot on the part of the Terrain Authority. I saw this almost at once. This mission is meant to fail," Harfex whispered to the Coordinator, glancing over his shoulder. Porlock was fumbling with his fly-button; there were tears in his eyes. I did tell you they were all crazy, but you thought I was exaggerating.

All the same, they were not unjustified. Extreme Surveyors expected to find their fellow team members intelligent, well trained, unstable, and personally sympathetic. They had to work together in close quarters, and nasty places, and could expect one another's paranoias, depressions, manias, phobias, and compulsions to be mild enough to admit of good personal relationship, at least most of the time. Osden might be intelligent, but his training was sketchy and his personality was disastrous. He had been sent only on account of his singular gift, the power of empathy: properly speaking, of wide-range bioemphatic receptivity. His talent wasn't species-specific; he could pick up emotion or sentience from anything that felt. He could share lust with a white rat, pain with a squashed cockroach, and phototropy with a moth. On an alien world, the Authority had decided, it would be useful to know if anything nearby is sentient, and if so, what its feelings towards you are. Osden's title was a new one: he was the team's Sensor.

"What is emotion, Osden?" Haito Tomiko asked him one day in the main cabin, trying to make some rapport with him for once. "What is it, exactly, that you pick up with your empathic sensitivity?"

"Muck," the man answered in his high, exasperated voice. "The psychic excreta of the animal kingdom. I wade through your faeces."

"I was trying," she said, "to learn some facts." She thought her tone was admirably calm.

"You weren't after facts. You were trying to get at me. With some fear, some curiosity, and a great deal of distaste. The way you might poke a dead dog, to see the maggots crawl. Will you understand once and for all that I don't want to be got at, that I want to be left alone?" His skin was mottled with red and violet, his voice had risen. "Go roll in your own dung, you yellow bitch!" he shouted at her silence.

"Calm down," she said, still quietly, but she left him at once and went to her cabin. Of course he had been right about her motives; her question had been largely

121

a pretext, a mere effort to interest him. But what harm in that? Did not that effort imply respect for the other? At the moment of asking the question she had felt at most a slight distrust of him; she had mostly felt sorry for him, the poor arrogant venomous bastard, Mr. No Skin as Olleroo called him. What did he expect, the way he acted? Love?

"I guess he can't stand anybody feeling sorry for him," said Olleroo, lying on the lower bunk, gilding her nipples.

"Then he can't form a human relationship. All his Dr. Hammergeld did was turn an autism inside out..."

"Poor frot," said Olleroo. "Tomiko, you don't mind if Harfex comes in for a while tonight, do you?"

"Can't you go to his cabin? I'm sick of always having to sit in Main with that damned peeled turnip."

"You do hate him, don't you? I guess he feels that. But I slept with Harfex last night too, and Asnanifoil might get jealous, since they share the cabin. It would be nicer here."

"Service them both," Tomiko said with the coarseness of offended modesty. Her Terran subculture, the East Asian, was a puritanical one; she had been brought up chaste.

"I only like one a night," Olleroo replied with innocent serenity. Beldene, the Garden Planet, had never discovered chastity, or the wheel.

"Try Osden, then," Tomiko said. Her personal instability was seldom so plain as now: a profound self-distrust manifesting itself as destructivism. She had volunteered for this job because there was, in all probability, no use in doing it.

The little Beldene looked up, paintbrush in hand, eyes wide. "Tomiko, that was a dirty thing to say."

"Why?"

"It would be vile! I'm not attracted to Osden!"

"I didn't know it mattered to you," Tomiko said indifferently, though she did know. She got some papers together and left the cabin, remarking, "I hope you and Harfex or whoever it is finish by last bell; I'm tired."

Olleroo was crying, tears dripping on her little gilded nipples. She wept easily. Tomiko had not wept since she was ten years old.

It was not a happy ship; but it took a turn for the better when Asnanifoil with his computer raised World 4470. There it lay, a dark-green jewel, like truth at the bottom of a gravity well. As they watched the jade disc grow, a sense of mutuality grew among them. Osden's selfishness, his accurate cruelty, served now to draw the others together. "Perhaps," Mannon said, "he was sent as a beating-gron. What Terrans call a scapegoat. Perhaps his influence will be good after all." And no one, so careful were they to be kind to one another, disagreed.

They came into orbit. There were no lights on nightside, on the continents none of the lines and clots made by animals who build.

"No men," Harfex murmured.

"Of course not," snapped Osden, who had a

viewscreen to himself, and his head inside a polythene bag. He claimed that the plastic cut down the empathic noise he received from the others. "We're two lightcenturies past the limit of the Hainish Expansion, and outside that there are no men. Anywhere. You don't think Creation would have made the same hideous mistake twice?"

No one was paying him much heed; they were looking with affection at that jade immensity below them, where there was life, but not human life. They were misfits among men, and what they saw there was not desolation, but peace. Even Osden did not look quite so expressionless as usual; he was frowning.

Descent in fire on the sea; air reconnaissance; landing. A plain of something like grass, thick, green, bowing stalks, surrounded the ship, brushed against extended view-cameras, smeared the lenses with a fine pollen.

"It looks like a pure phytosphere," Harfex said. "Osden, do you pick up anything sentient?"

They all turned to the Sensor. He had left the screen and was pouring himself a cup of tea. He did not answer. He seldom answered spoken questions.

The chitinous rigidity of military discipline was quite inapplicable to these teams of Mad Scientists; their chain of command lay somewhere between parliamentary procedure and peck-order, and would have driven a regular service officer out of his mind. By the inscrutable decision of the Authority, however, Dr. Haito Tomiko had been given the title of Coordinator, and she now exercised her prerogative for the first time.

"Mr. Sensor Osden," she said, "please answer Mr. Harfex."

"How could I 'pick up' anything from outside," Osden said without turning, "with the emotions of nine neurotic hominids pullulating around me like worms in a can? When I have anything to tell you, I'll tell you. I'm aware of my responsibility as Sensor. If you presume to give me an order again, however, Coordinator Haito, I'll consider my responsibility void."

"Very well, Mr. Sensor. I trust no orders will be needed henceforth." Tomiko's bullfrog voice was calm, but Osden seemed to flinch slightly as he stood with his back to her: as if the surge of her suppressed rancor had struck him with physical force.

The biologist's hunch proved correct. When they began field analyses they found no animals even among the microbiota. Nobody here ate anybody else. All life-forms were photosynthesizing or saprophagous, living off light or death, not off life. Plants: infinite plants, not one species known to the visitors from the house of Man. Infinite shades and intensities of green, violet, purple, brown, red. Infinite silences. Only the wind moved, swaying leaves and fronds, a warm soughing wind laden with spores and pollens, blowing the sweet pale-green dust over prairies of great grasses, heaths that bore no heather, flowerless forests where no foot had ever walked, no eye had ever looked. A warm, sad world, sad and serene.

The Surveyors, wandering like picnickers over sunny plains of violet filicaliformes, spoke softly to each other.

They knew their voices broke a silence of a thousand million years, the silence of wind and leaves, leaves and wind, blowing and ceasing and blowing again. They talked softly; but being human, they talked.

"Poor old Osden," said Jenny Chong, Bio and Tech, as she piloted a helijet on the North Polar Quadrating run. "All that fancy hi-fi stuff in his brain and nothing to receive. What a bust."

"He told me he hates plants," Olleroo said with a giggle.

"You'd think he'd like them, since they don't bother him like we do."

"Can't say I much like these plants myself," said Porlock, looking down at the purple undulations of the North Circumpolar Forest. "All the same. No mind. No change. A man alone in it would go right off his head."

"But it's all alive," Jenny Chong said. "And if it lives, Osden hates it."

"He's not really so bad," Olleroo said, magnanimous. Porlock looked at her sidelong and asked, "You ever slept with him, Olleroo?"

Olleroo burst into tears and cried, "You Terrans are obscene!"

"No she hasn't," Jenny Chong said, prompt to defend. "Have you, Porlock?"

The chemist laughed uneasily: Ha, ha, ha. Flecks of spittle appeared on his mustache.

"Osden can't bear to be touched," Olleroo said shakily. "I just brushed against him once by accident and he knocked me off like I was some sort of dirty... thing. We're all just things, to him."

"He's evil," Porlock said in a strained voice, startling the two women. "He'll end up shattering this team, sabotaging it, one way or another. Mark my words. He's not fit to live with other people!"

They landed on the North Pole. A midnight sun smouldered over low hills. Short. dry, greenish-pink bryoform grasses stretched away in every direction, which was all one direction, south. Subdued by the incredible silence, the three Surveyors set up their instruments and collected their samples, three viruses twitching minutely on the hide of an unmoving giant.

Nobody asked Osden along on runs as pilot or photographer or recorder, and he never volunteered, so he seldom left base camp. He ran Harfex's botanical taxonomic data through the on-ship computers, and served as assistant to Eskwana, whose job here was mainly repair and maintenance. Eskwana had begun to sleep a great deal, twenty-five hours or more out of the thirty-two hour day, dropping off in the middle of repairing a radio or checking the guidance circuits of a helijet. The Coordinator stayed at base one day to observe. No one else was home except Poswet To, who was subject to epileptic fits; Mannon had plugged her into a therapycircuit today in a state of preventive catatonia. Tomiko spoke reports into the storage banks, and kept an eye on Osden and Eskwana. Two hours passed.

"You might want to use the 860 microwaldoes in sealing that connection," Eskwana said in his soft, hesitant voice.

"Obviously!"

"Sorry. I just saw you had the 840s there—"

"And will replace them when I take the 860s out. When I don't know how to proceed, Engineer, I'll ask your advice."

After a minute Tomiko looked round. Sure enough, there was Eskwana sound asleep, head on the table, thumb in his mouth.

"Osden."

The white face did not turn, he did not speak, but conveyed impatiently that he was listening.

"You can't be unaware of Eskwana's vulnerability."

"I am not responsible for his psychopathic reactions."

"But you are responsible for your own. Eskwana is essential to our work, here, and you're not. If you can't control your hostility, you must avoid him altogether."

Osden put down his tools and stood up. "With pleasure!" he said in his vindictive, scraping voice. "You could not possibly imagine what it's like to *experience* Eskwana's irrational terrors. To have to share his horrible cowardice, to have to cringe with him at everything!"

"Are you trying to justify your cruelty towards him? I thought you had more self-respect," Tomiko found herself shaking with spite. "If your empathic power really makes you share Ander's misery, why does it never induce the least compassion in you?"

"Compassion," Osden said. "Compassion. What do you know about compassion?"

She stared at him, but he would not look at her. "Would you like me to verbalize your present emotional affect regarding myself?" he said. "I can do so more precisely than you can. I'm trained to analyze such responses as I receive them. And I do receive them."

"But how can you expect me to feel kindly towards you when you behave as you do?"

"What does it matter how I *behave*, you stupid sow, do you think it makes any difference? Do you think the average human is a well of loving kindness? My choice is to be hated or to be despised. Not being a woman or a coward, I prefer to be hated."

"That's rot. Self-pity. Every man has—"

"But I am not a man," Osden said. "There are all of you. And there is myself. I am *one*".

Awed by that glimpse of abysmal solipsism, she kept silent a while; finally she said with neither spite nor pity, clinically, "You could kill yourself, Osden."

"That's your way, Haito," he jeered. "I'm not depressive and *seppuku* isn't my bit. What do you want me to do here?"

"Leave. Spare yourself and us. Take the aircar and a data-feeder and go do a species count. In the forest; Harfex hasn't even started the forests yet. Take a hundred-square-meter forested area, anywhere inside radio range. But outside empathy range. Report in at eight and twenty-four o'clock daily."

Osden went, and nothing was heard from him for five days but laconic all-well signals twice daily. The mood at base camp changed like a stage set. Eskwana stayed awake up to eighteen hours a day. Poswet To got out her stellar lute and chanted the celestial harmonies (music had driven Osden to frenzy). Mannon, Harfex, Jenny Chong, and Tomiko all went off tranquilizers. Porlock distilled something in his laboratory and drank it all by himself. He had a hangover. Asnanifoil and Poswet To held an all-night Numerical Epiphany, that mystical orgy of higher mathematics which is the chiefest pleasure of the religious Cetian soul. Olleroo slept with everybody. Work went well.

The Hard Scientist came towards base at a run, laboring through the high, fleshy stalks of the graminiformes. "Something—in the forest—" His eyes bulged, he panted, his mustache and fingers trembled. "Something big. Moving, behind me. I was putting in a bench-mark, bending down. It came at me. As if it was swinging down out of the trees. Behind me." He stared at the others with the opaque eyes of terror or exhaustion.

"Sit down, Porlock. Take it easy. Now wait, go through this again. You *saw* something—"

"Not clearly. Just the movement. Purposive. A—an—I don't know what it could have been. Something self-moving. In the trees, the arboriformes, whatever you call 'em. At the edge of the woods."

Harfex looked grim. "There is nothing here that could attack you, Porlock. There are not even microzoa.

There *could not* be a large animal."

"Could you possibly have seen an epiphyte drop suddenly, a vine come loose behind you?"

"No," Porlock said. "It was coming down at me, through the branches, fast. When I turned it took off again, away and upward. It made a noise, a sort of crashing. If it wasn't an animal, God knows what it could have been! It was big—as big as a man, at least. Maybe a reddish color. I couldn't see, I'm not sure,"

"It was Osden." said Jenny Chong, "doing a Tarzan act." She giggled nervously, and Tomiko repressed a wild reckless laugh. But Harfex was not smiling.

"One gets uneasy under the arboriformes," he said in his polite, repressed voice. "I've noticed that. Indeed that may be why I've put off working in the forests. There's a hypnotic quality in the colors and spacing of the stems and branches, especially the helically arranged ones; and the spore-throwers grow so regularly spaced that it seems unnatural. I find it quite disagreeable, subjectively speaking. I wonder if a stronger effect of that sort mightn't have produced a hallucination...?"

Porlock shook his head. He wet his lips. "It was there," he said. "Something. Moving with purpose. Trying to attack me from behind."

When Osden called in, punctual as always, at twenty-four o'clock that night, Harfex told him Porlock's report. "Have you come on anything at all, Mr. Osden, that could substantiate Mr. Porlock's impression of a motile, sentient life-form, in the forest?"

131

Ssss, the radio said sardonically. "No. Bullshit," said Osden's unpleasant voice.

"You've been actually inside the forest longer than any of us," Harfex said with unmitigable politeness. "Do you agree with my impression that the forest ambiance has a rather troubling and possibly hallucinogenic effect on the perceptions?"

Ssss. "I'll agree that Porlock's perceptions are easily troubled. Keep him in his lab, he'll do less harm. Anything else?"

"Not at present," Harfex said, and Osden cut off. Nobody could credit Porlock's story, and nobody could discredit it. He was positive that something, something big, had tried to attack him by surprise, It was hard to deny this, for they were on an alien world, and everyone who had entered the forest had felt a certain chill and foreboding under the "trees." ("Call them trees, certainly," Harfex had said: "They really are the same thing, only, of course, altogether different.") They agreed that they had felt uneasy, or had had the sense that something was watching them from behind.

"We've got to clear this up," Porlock said, and he asked to be sent as a temporary Biologist's Aide, like Osden, into the forest to explore and observe. Olleroo and Jenny Chong volunteered if they could go as a pair. Harfex sent them all off into the forest near which they were encamped, a vast tract covering four-fifths of Continent D. He forbade side arms. They were not to go outside a fifty-kilo half-circle, which included Osden's current site.

They all reported in twice daily, for three days. Porlock reported a glimpse of what seemed to be a large semi-erect shape moving through the trees across the river; Olleroo was sure she had heard something moving near the tent, the second night.

"There are no animals on this planet," Harfex said, dogged.

Then Osden missed his morning call.

Tomiko waited less than an hour, then flew with Harfex to the area where Osden had reported himself the night before. But as the helijet hovered over the sea of purplish leaves, illimitable, impenetrable, she felt a panic despair. "How can we find him in this?"

"He reported landing on the river bank. Find the air-car; he'll be camped near it, and he can't have gone far from his camp. Species-counting is slow work. There's the river."

"There's his car," Tomiko said, catching the bright foreign glint among the vegetable colors and shadows. "Here goes, then."

She put the ship in hover and pitched out the ladder. She and Harfex descended. The sea of life closed over their heads.

As her feet touched the forest floor, she unsnapped the flap of her holster; then glancing at Harfex, who was un-armed, she left the gun untouched. But her hand kept coming back up to it. There was no sound at all, as soon as they were a few meters away from the slow, brown river, and the light was dim. Great boles stood well apart, almost regularly, almost alike; they were soft-skinned, some appearing smooth and others spongy, gray or greenish-brown or brown, twined with cablelike creepers and festooned with epiphytes, extending rigid, entangled armfuls of big, saucer-shaped, dark leaves that formed a roof-layer twenty to thirty meters thick. The ground underfoot was springy as a mattress, every inch of it knotted with roots and peppered with small, fleshy-leaved growths.

"Here's his tent," Tomiko said, cowed at the sound of her voice in that huge community of the voiceless. In the tent was Osden's sleeping bag, a couple of books, a box of rations. We should be calling, shouting for him, she thought, but did not even suggest it; nor did Harfex. They circled out from the tent, careful to keep each other in sight through the thick-standing presences, the crowding gloom. She stumbled over Osden's body, not thirty meters from the tent, led to it by the whitish gleam of a dropped notebook. He lay face down between two huge-rooted trees. His head and hands were covered with blood, some dried, some still oozing red.

Harfex appeared beside her, his pale Hainish complexion quite green in the dusk. "Dead?"

"No. He's been struck. Beaten. From behind." Tomiko's fingers felt over the bloody skull and nape and temples. "A weapon or a tool... I don't find a fracture."

As she turned Osden's body over so they could lift him, his eyes opened. She was holding him, bending close to his face. His pale lips writhed. A deathly fear came to her. She screamed aloud two or three times

134

and tried to run away, shambling and stumbling into the terrible dusk. Harfex caught her, and at his touch and the sound of his voice, her panic decreased. "What is it? What is it?" he was saying.

"I don't know," she sobbed. Her heartbeat still shook her, and she could not see clearly. "The fear— the... I panicked. When I saw his eyes."

"We're both nervous. I don't understand this—"

"I'm all right now, come on, we've got to get him under care."

Both working with senseless haste, they lugged Osden to the riverside and hauled him up on a rope under his armpits; he dangled like a sack, twisting a little, over the glutinous dark sea of leaves. They pulled him into the helijet and took off. Within a minute they were over open prairie. Tomiko locked onto the homing beam. She drew a deep breath, and her eyes met Harfex's.

"I was so terrified I almost fainted. I have never done that."

"I was... unreasonably frightened also," said the Hainishman, and indeed he looked aged and shaken. "Not so badly as you. But as unreasonably."

"It was when I was in contact with him, holding him. He seemed to be conscious for a moment."

"Empathy?... I hope he can tell us what attacked him."

Osden, like a broken dummy covered with blood and mud, half-lay as they had bundled him into the rear seats in their frantic urgency to get out of the forest.

More panic met their arrival at base. The ineffective brutality of the assault was sinister and bewildering.

Since Harfex stubbornly denied any possibility of animal life they began speculating about sentient plants, vegetable monsters, psychic projections. Jenny Chong's latent phobia reasserted itself and she could talk about nothing except the Dark Egos which followed people around behind their backs. She and Olleroo and Porlock had been summoned back to base; and nobody was much inclined to go outside.

Osden had lost a good deal of blood during the three or four hours he had lain alone, and concussion and severe contusions had put him in shock and semi-coma. As he came out of this and began running a lower fever he called several times for "Doctor," in a plaintive voice: "Doctor Hammergeld..." When he regained full consciousness, two of those long days later, Tomiko called Harfex into the cubicle.

"Osden: can you tell us what attacked you?" The pale eyes flickered past Harfex's face.

"You were attacked," Tomiko said gently. The shifty gaze was hatefully familiar, but she was a physician, protective of the hurt. "You may not remember it yet. Something attacked you. You were in the forest—"

"Ah!" he cried out, his eyes growing bright and his features contorting. "The forest—in the forest—"

"What's in the forest?"

He gasped for breath. A look of clearer consciousness came into his face. After a while he said, "I don't know."

"Did you see what attacked you?" Harfex asked.

"I don't know."

"You remember it now."

"I don't know."

"All our lives may depend on this. You must tell us what you saw!"

"I don't know," Osden said, sobbing with weakness. He was too weak to hide the fact that he was hiding the answer, yet he would not say it. Porlock, nearby, was chewing his pepper-colored mustache as he tried to bear what was going on in the cubicle. Harfex leaned over Osden and said, "You *will* tell us—" Tomiko had to interfere bodily.

Harfex controlled himself with an effort that was painful to see. He went off silently to his cubicle, where no doubt he took a double or triple dose of tranquilizers. The other men and women, scattered about the big frail building, a long main hall and ten sleeping-cubicles, said nothing, but looked depressed and edgy. Osden, as always, even now, had them all at his mercy. Tomiko looked down at him with a rush of hatred that burned in her throat like bile. This monstrous egotism that fed itself on others' emotions, this absolute selfishness, was worse than any hideous deformity of the flesh. Like a congenital monster, he should not have lived. Should not be alive. Should have died. Why had his head not been split open?

As he lay flat and white, his hands helpless at his sides, his colorless eyes were wide open, and there were tears running from the corners. Tomiko moved

towards him suddenly. He tried to flinch away. "Don't,"
he said in a weak hoarse voice, and tried to raise his
hands to protect his head. "Don't!"

She sat down on the folding stool beside the cot, and
after a while put her hand on his. He tried to pull away,
but lacked the strength.

A long silence fell between them.

"Osden," she murmured. "I'm sorry. I'm very sorry.
I will you well. Let me will you well, Osden. I don't want
to hurt you. Listen, I do see now. It was one of us. That's
right, isn't it. No, don't answer, only tell me if I'm wrong;
but I'm not... Of course there are animals on this planet:
Ten of them. I don't care who it was. It doesn't matter,
does it. It could have been me, just now. I realize that.
I didn't understand how it is, Osden. You can't see how
difficult it is for us to understand... But listen. If it were
love, instead of hate and fear... Is it never love?"

"No."

"Why not? Why should it never be? Are human
beings all so weak? That is terrible. Never mind, never
mind, don't worry. Keep still. At least right now it isn't
hate, is it? Sympathy at least, concern, well-wishing.
You do feel that, Osden? Is it what you feel?"

"Among... other things," he said, almost inaudible.
"Noise from my subconscious, I suppose. And everybody else in the room... Listen, when we found you
there in the forest, when I tried to turn you over, you
partly wakened, and I felt a horror of you. I was insane
with fear for a minute. Was that your fear of me I felt?"

"No."

Her hand was still on his, and he was quite relaxed, sinking towards sleep, like a man in pain who has been given relief from pain. "The forest," he muttered; she could barely understand him. "Afraid."

She pressed him no further, but kept her hand on his and watched him go to sleep. She knew what she felt, and what therefore he must feel. She was confident of it: there is only one emotion, or state of being, that can thus wholly reverse itself, polarize, within one moment. In Great Hainish indeed there is one word, *ontá*, for love and for hate. She was not in love with Osden, of course, that is another kettle of fish. What she felt for him was *ontá*, polarized hate. She held his hand and the current flowed between them, the tremendous electricity of touch, which he had always dreaded. As he slept the ring of anatomy-chart muscles around his mouth relaxed, and Tomiko saw on his face what none of them had ever seen, very faint, a smile. It faded. He slept on.

He was tough; next day he was sitting up, and hungry. Harfex wished to interrogate him, but Tomiko put him off. She hung a sheet of polythene over the cubicle door, as Osden himself had often done. "Does it actually cut down your empathic reception?" she asked, and he replied, in the dry, cautious tone they were now using to each other, "No."

"Just a warning, then."

"Partly. More faith-healing. Dr. Hammergeld thought it worked... Maybe it does, a little."

There had been love, once. A terrified child, suffocating in the tidal rush and battering of the huge emotions of adults, a drowning child, saved by one man. Taught to breathe, to live, by one man. Given everything, all protection and love, by one man. Father/mother/God: no other. "Is he still alive?" Tomiko said, thinking of Osden's incredible loneliness, and the savage cruelty of the great doctors. She was shocked when she heard his forced, tinny laugh. "He died at least two and a half centuries ago," Osden said. "Do you forget where we are, Coordinator? We've all left our little families behind…"

Outside the polythene curtain the eight other human beings on World 4470 moved vaguely. Their voices were low and strained. Eskwana slept; Poswet To was in therapy; Jenny Chong was trying to rig lights in her cubicle so that she wouldn't cast a shadow.

"They're all scared," Tomiko said, scared. "They've all got these ideas about what attacked you. A sort of ape-potato, a giant fanged spinach, I don't know… Even Harfex. You may be right not to force them to see. That would be worse, to lose confidence in one another. But why are we all so shaky, unable to face the fact, going to pieces so easily? Are we really all insane?"

"We'll soon be more so."

"Why?"

"There *is* something."

He closed his mouth, the muscles of his lips stood out rigid.

"Something sentient?"

"A sentience."

"In the forest?" He nodded.

"What is it, then—?"

"The fear." He began to look strained again, and moved restlessly. "When I fell, there, you know, I didn't lose consciousness at once. Or I kept regaining it. I don't know. It was more like being paralyzed."

"You were."

"I was on the ground. I couldn't get up. My face was in the dirt, in that soft leafmold. It was in my nostrils and eyes. I couldn't move. Couldn't see. As if I was in the ground. Sunk into it, part of it. I knew I was between two trees even though I never saw them. I suppose I could feel the roots. Below me in the ground, down under the ground. My hands were bloody, I could feel that, and the blood made the dirt around my face sticky. I felt the fear. It kept growing. As if they'd finally *known* I was there, lying on them there, under them, among them, the thing they feared, and yet part of their fear itself. I couldn't stop sending the fear back, and it kept growing, and I couldn't move, I couldn't get away. I would pass out, I think, and then the fear would bring me to again, and I still couldn't move. Any more than they can."

Tomiko felt the cold stirring of her hair, the readying of the apparatus of terror. "They: who are *they*, Osden?"

"They, it—I don't know. The fear."

"What is he talking about?" Harfex demanded when Tomiko reported this conversation. She would not let Harfex question Osden yet, feeling that she must

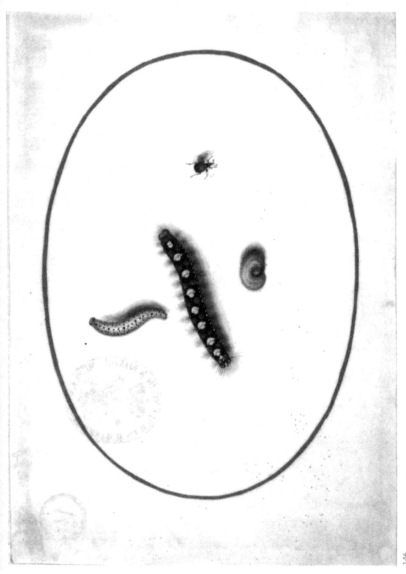

Three caterpillars and small beetle, in transverse oval with gold edge, circa 1770.

protect Osden from the onslaught of the Hainishman's powerful, over-repressed emotions. Unfortunately this fueled the slow fire of paranoid anxiety that burned in poor Harfex, and he thought she and Osden were in league, hiding some fact of great importance or peril from the rest of the team.

"It's like the blind man trying to describe the elephant. Osden hasn't seen or heard the... the sentience, any more than we have."

"But he's felt it, my dear Haito," Harfex said with just-suppressed rage. "Not empathically. On his skull. It came and knocked him down and beat him with a blunt instrument. Did he not catch *one* glimpse of it?"

"What would he have seen, Harfex?" Tomiko asked, but he would not hear her meaningful tone; even he had blocked out that comprehension. What one fears is alien. The murderer is an outsider, a foreigner, not one of us. The evil is not in me!

"The first blow knocked him pretty well out," Tomiko said a little wearily, "he didn't see anything. But when he came to again, alone in the forest, he felt a great fear. Not his own fear, an empathic affect. He is certain of that. And certain it was nothing picked up from any of us. So that evidently the native life-forms are not all insentient."

Harfex looked at her a moment, grim. "You're trying to frighten me, Haito. I do not understand your motives." He got up and went off to his laboratory table, walking slowly and stiffly, like a man of eighty not of forty.

She looked round at the others. She felt some desperation. Her new, fragile, and profound interdependence with Osden gave her, she was well aware, some added strength. But if even Harfex could not keep his head, who of the others would? Porlock and Eskwana were shut in their cubicles, the others were all working or busy with something. There was something queer about their positions. For a while the Coordinator could not tell what it was, then she saw that they were all sitting facing the nearby forest. Playing chess with Asnanifoil, Olleroo had edged her chair around until it was almost beside his.

She went to Mannon, who was dissecting a tangle of spidery brown roots, and told him to look for the pattern-puzzle. He saw it at once, and said with unusual brevity, "Keeping an eye on the enemy."

"What enemy? What do *you* feel, Mannon?" She had a sudden hope in him as a psychologist, on this obscure ground of hints and empathies where biologists went astray.

"I feel a strong anxiety with a specific spatial orientation. But I am not an empath. Therefore, the anxiety is explicable in terms of the particular stress-situation, that is the attack on a team member in the forest, and also in terms of the total stress-situation, that is my presence in a totally alien environment, for which the archetypical connotations of the word 'forest' provide an inevitable metaphor."

Hours later Tomiko woke to hear Osden screaming in nightmare; Mannon was calming him, and she sank back into her own dark-branching pathless dreams. In the morning Eskwana did not wake. He could not be roused with stimulant drugs. He clung to his sleep, slipping farther and farther back, mumbling softly now and then until, wholly regressed, he lay curled on his side, thumb at his lips, gone.

"Two days: two down. Ten little Indians, nine little Indians..." That was Porlock.

"And you're the next little Indian," Jenny Chong snapped. "Go analyze your urine, Porlock!"

"He is driving us all insane," Porlock said, getting up and waving his left arm. "Can't you feel it? For God's sake, are you all deaf and blind? Can't you feel what he's doing, the emanations? It all comes from him—from his room there—from his mind. He is driving us all insane with fear!"

"Who is?" said Asnanifoil, looming black, precipitous and hairy over the little Terran.

"Do I have to say his name? Osden, then. Osden! Osden! Why do you think I tried to kill him? In self-defense! To save all of us! Because you won't see what he's doing to us. He's sabotaged the mission by making us quarrel, and now he's going to drive us all insane by projecting fear at us so that we can't sleep or think, like a huge radio that doesn't make any sound, but it broadcasts all the time, and you can't sleep, and you can't think. Haito and Harfex are already under his control but the rest of you can be saved. I had to do it!"

"You didn't do it very well," Osden said, standing half-naked, all rib and bandage, at the door of his cubicle. "I could have hit myself harder. Hell, it isn't me that's scaring you blind, Porlock, it's out there—there, in the woods!"

Porlock made an ineffectual attempt to assault Osden; Asnanifoil held him back, and continued to hold him effortlessly while Mannon gave him a sedative shot. He was put away shouting about giant radios. In a minute the sedative took effect, and he joined a peaceful silence to Eskwana's.

"All right," said Harfex. "Now, by my Gods, you'll tell us what you know and all you know."

Osden said, "I don't know anything."

He looked battered and faint. Tomiko made him sit down before he talked.

"After I'd been three days in the forest, I thought I was occasionally receiving some kind of faint affect." "Why didn't you report it?"

"Thought I was going spla, like the rest of you."

"That, equally, should have been reported."

"You'd have called me back to base. I couldn't take it. You realize that my inclusion in the mission was a bad mistake. I'm not able to coexist with nine other neurotic personalities at close quarters. I was wrong to volunteer for Extreme Survey, and the Authority was wrong to accept me."

No one spoke; but Tomiko saw, with certainty this time, the flinch in Osden's shoulders and the tightening of his facial muscles, as he registered their bitter agreement. "Anyhow, I didn't want to come back to base, because I was curious. Even going psycho, how could I pick up empathic affects when there was no creature to emit them? They weren't bad, then. Very vague. Queer. Like a draft in a closed room, a flicker in the corner of your eye. Nothing really."

For a moment he had been borne up on their listening: they heard, so he spoke. He was wholly at their mercy. If they disliked him, he had to be hateful; if they mocked him he became grotesque; if they listened to him he was the storyteller. He was helplessly obedient to the demands of their emotions, reactions, moods. And there were seven of them, too many to cope with, so that he must be constantly knocked about from one to another's whim. He could not find coherence. Even as he spoke and held them, somebody's attention would wander: Olleroo perhaps was thinking that he wasn't unattractive; Harfex was seeking the ulterior motive of his words; Asnanifoil's mind, which could not be long held by the concrete, was roaming off towards the eternal peace of number; and Tomiko was distracted by pity, by fear. Osden's voice faltered. He lost the thread.

"I... I thought it must be the trees," he said, and stopped.

"It's not the trees," Harfex said. "They have no more nervous system than do plants of the Hainish Descent on Earth. None."

"You're not seeing the forest for the trees, as they say on Earth," Mannon put in, smiling elfinly; Harfex stared at him. "What about those root-nodes we've been puzzling about for twenty days—eh?"

"What about them?"

"They are, indubitably, connections. Connections among the trees. Right? Now let's just suppose, most improbably, that you knew nothing of animal brainstructure. And you were given one axon, or one detached glial cell, to examine. Would you be likely to discover what it was? Would you see that the cell was capable of sentience?"

"No. Because it isn't. A single cell is capable of mechanical response to stimulus. No more. Are you hypothesizing that individual arboriformes are 'cells' in a kind of brain, Mannon?"

"Not exactly. I'm merely pointing out that they are all interconnected, both by the root-node linkage and by your green epiphytes in the branches. A linkage of incredible complexity and physical extent. Why, even the prairie grass-forms have those root-connectors, don't they? I know that sentience or intelligence isn't a thing, you can't find it in, or analyze it out from, the cells of a brain. It's a function of the connected cells. It is, in a sense, the connection: the connectedness. It doesn't exist. I'm not trying to say it exists. I'm only guessing that Osden might be able to describe it."

And Osden took him up, speaking as if in trance. "Sentience without senses. Blind, deaf, nerveless, moveless. Some irritability, response to touch. Response to sun, to light, to water, and chemicals in the earth around the roots. Nothing comprehensible to an animal mind. Presence without mind. Awareness of being, without object or subject. Nirvana."

"Then why do you receive fear?" Tomiko asked in a low voice.

"I don't know. I can't see how awareness of objects, of others, could arise: an unperceiving response... But there was an uneasiness, for days. And then when I lay between the two trees and my blood was on their roots—" Osden's face glittered with sweat. "It became fear," he said shrilly, "only fear."

"If such a function existed," Harfex said, "it would not be capable of conceiving of a self-moving, material entity, or responding to one. It could no more become aware of us than we can 'become aware' of Infinity."

"The silence of those infinite expanses terrifies me," muttered Tomiko. "Pascal was aware of Infinity. By way of fear."

"To a forest," Mannon said, "we might appear as forest fires. Hurricanes. Dangers. What moves quickly is dangerous, to a plant. The rootless would be alien, terrible. And if it is mind, it seems only too probable that it might become aware of Osden, whose own mind is open to connection with all others so long as he's conscious, and who was lying in pain and afraid within it, actually inside it. No wonder it was afraid—"

"Not 'it,'" Harfex said. "There is no being, no huge creature, no person! There could at most be only a function—"

"There is only a fear," Osden said.

They were all still a while, and heard the stillness outside.

"Is that what I feel all the time coming up behind me?" Jenny Chong asked, subdued.

Osden nodded. "You all feel it, deaf as you are. Eskwana's the worst off, because he actually has some empathic capacity. He could send if he learned how, but he's too weak, never will be anything but a medium."

"Listen, Osden," Tomiko said, "you can send. Then send to it—the forest, the fear out there—tell it that we won't hurt it. Since it has, or is, some sort of affect that translates into what we feel as emotion, can't you translate back? Send out a message, We are harmless, we are friendly."

"You must know that nobody can emit a false empathic message, Haito. You can't send something that doesn't exist."

"But we don't intend harm, we are friendly."

"Are we? In the forest, when you picked me up, did you feel friendly?"

"No. Terrified. But that's—it, the forest, the plants, not my own fear, isn't it?"

"What's the difference? It's all you felt. Can't you see," and Osden's voice rose in exasperation, "why I dislike you and you dislike me, all of you? Can't you see that I retransmit every negative or aggressive affect you've felt towards me since we first met? I return your hostility, with thanks. I do it in self-defense. Like Porlock. It is self-defense, though, it's the only technique I developed to replace my original defense of total withdrawal from others. Unfortunately it creates a closed circuit, self-sustaining and self-reinforcing. Your initial reaction

150

to me was the instinctive antipathy to a cripple; by now of course it's hatred. Can you fail to see my point? The forest-mind out there transmits only terror, now, and the only message I can send it is terror, because when exposed to it I can feel nothing except terror!"

"What must we do, then?" said Tomiko, and Mannon replied promptly, "Move camp. To another continent. If there are plant-minds there, they'll be slow to notice us, as this one was; maybe they won't notice us at all."

"It would be a considerable relief," Osden observed stiffly. The others had been watching him with a new curiosity. He had revealed himself, they had seen him as he was, a helpless man in a trap. Perhaps, like Tomiko, they had seen that the trap itself, his crass and cruel egotism, was their own construction, not his. They had built the cage and locked him in it, and like a caged ape he threw filth out through the bars. If, meeting him, they had offered trust, if they had been strong enough to offer him love, how might he have appeared to them?

None of them could have done so, and it was too late now. Given time, given solitude, Tomiko might have built up with him a slow resonance of feeling, a consonance of trust, a harmony: but there was no time, their job must be done. There was not room enough for the cultivation of so great a thing, and they must make do with sympathy, with pity, the small change of love. Even that much had given her strength, but it was nowhere near enough for him. She could see in his flayed face now his savage resentment of their curiosity, even of her pity.

P. 178

In the 1960s, much ceremonial life had been suppressed in the encounter with colonial officers and missionaries bent on putting an end to the consumption of deceased relatives and the rituals and ideas associated with the practice.

P. 83

Government and mission edicts quickly brought a halt to warfare, cannibalism, and – for the next decade – to most indigenous ritual. The New World Mission would not baptize new polygamists. The Seventh Day Adventists refused those who ate pork, possum, rats, or snakes. Government representatives discouraged infanticide and child marriage, and the missions forbade the traditional privilege of premarital sex with matrilateral cross-cousins. Lutheran missionaries... made occasional visits, during which they undermined indigenous beliefs by revealing the men's sacred flutes to women. Lutheran baptism also required monogamy, and while the World Mission allowed current polygamists to keep all their wives, the Lutherans insisted on the divorce of all but one.

P. 83

Domestic architecture soon reflected the new era. The stockades surrounding South Fore hamlets were pulled down in 1956, and houses were built in open clearings where individual nuclear families settled side by side in suburban-style rows.

P. 171

The elders at Waisa remember the first missionaries telling them to cast off old ways, and to stop performing magic and sorcery. People sold their shields, weapons, and working tools, and turned away from old customs, including initiation. As [Ronald] Berndt noted, however, the pig exchanges may have disappeared, but the dominant values of the belief system still remained...

"Go lie down, that gash is bleeding again," she said, and he obeyed her.

Next morning they packed up, melted down the spray-form hangar and living quarters, lifted *Gum* on mechanical drive and took her halfway round World 4470, over the red and green lands, the many warm-green seas. They had picked out a likely spot on Continent G: a prairie, twenty thousand square kilos of windswept graminiformes. No forest was within a hundred kilos of the site, and there were no lone trees or groves on the plain. The plant-forms occurred only in large species-colonies, never intermingled, except for certain tiny ubiquitous saprophytes and spore-bearers. The team sprayed holomeld over structure forms, and by evening of the thirty-two-hour day were settled in to the new camp. Eskwana was still asleep and Porlock still sedated, but everyone else was cheerful. "You can breathe here!" they kept saying.

Osden got on his feet and went shakily to the doorway; leaning there he looked through twilight over the dim reaches of the swaying grass that was not grass. There was a faint, sweet odor of pollen on the wind; no sound but the soft, vast sibilance of wind. His bandaged head cocked a little, the empath stood motionless for a long time. Darkness came, and the stars, lights in the windows of the distant house of Man. The wind had ceased, there was no sound. He listened.

In the long night Haito Tomiko listened. She lay still and heard the blood in her arteries, the breathing of sleepers, the wind blowing, the dark veins running, the dreams advancing, the vast static of stars increasing as the universe died slowly, the sound of death walking. She struggled out of her bed, fled the tiny solitude of her cubicle. Eskwana alone slept. Porlock lay straitjacketed, raving softly in his obscure native tongue. Olleroo and Jenny Chong were playing cards, grim-faced. Poswet To was in the therapy niche, plugged in. Asnanifoil was drawing a mandala, the Third Pattern of the Primes. Mannon and Harfex were sitting up with Osden.

She changed the bandages on Osden's head. His lank, reddish hair, where she had not had to shave it, looked strange. It was salted with white, now. Her hands shook as she worked. Nobody had yet said anything.

"How can the fear be here too?" she said, and her voice rang flat and false in the terrific silence of the vegetable night.

"It's not just the trees: the grasses too..."

"But we're twelve thousand kilos from where we were this morning, we left it on the other side of the planet."

"It's all one," Osden said. "One big green thought. How long does it take a thought to get from one side of your brain to the other?"

"It doesn't think. It isn't thinking." Harfex said, life-lessly. "It's merely a network of processes. The branches, the epiphytic growths, the roots with those nodal junctures between individuals: they must all be capable of transmitting electrochemical impulses. There are no individual plants, then, properly speaking. Even the pollen is part of the linkage, no doubt, a sort of windborne sentience, connecting overseas. But it is not conceivable. That all the biosphere of a planet should be one network of communications, sensitive, irrational, immortal, isolated..."

"Isolated," said Osden. "That's it! That's the fear. It isn't that we're motile, or destructive. It's just that we are. We are other. There has never been any other."

"You're right," Mannon said, almost whispering. "It has no peers. No enemies. No relationship with anything but itself. One alone forever."

"Then what's its function in species-survival?"

"None, maybe," Osden said. "Why are you getting teleological, Harfex? Aren't you a Hainishman? Isn't the measure of complexity the measure of the eternal joy?"

Harfex did not take the bait. He looked ill. "We should leave this world," he said.

"Now you know why I always want to get out, get away from you," Osden said with a kind of morbid geniality. "It isn't pleasant, is it—the other's fear?... If only it were an animal intelligence. I can get through to animals. I get along with cobras and tigers; superior intelligence gives one the advantage. I should have been used in a zoo, not on a human team.... If I could get through to the damned stupid potato! If it wasn't so overwhelming....I still pick up more than the fear, you know. And before it panicked it had a—there was a serenity. I couldn't take it in, then, I didn't realize how big it was. To know the whole daylight, after all, and the whole night. All the winds and the lulls together. The winter stars and the summer stars at the same time. To have roots, and no enemies. To be entire. Do you see? No invasion. No others. To be whole...."

He had never spoken before, Tomiko thought. "You are defenseless against it, Osden," she said. "Your personality has changed already. You're vulnerable to it. We may not all go mad, but you will, if we don't leave."

He hesitated, then he looked up at Tomiko, the first time he had ever met her eyes, a long, still look, clear as water.

"What's sanity ever done for me?" he said, mocking. "But you have a point, Haito. You have something there."

"We should get away," Harfex muttered.

"If I gave in to it," Osden mused, "could I communicate?"

"By 'give in,'" Mannon said in a rapid, nervous voice, "I assume that you mean, stop sending back the empathic information which you receive from the plant-entity: stop rejecting the fear, and absorb it. That will either kill you at once, or drive you back into total psychological withdrawal, autism."

"Why?" said Osden. "Its message is *rejection*.

But my salvation is rejection. It's not intelligent. But I am."

"The scale is wrong. What can a single human brain achieve against something so vast?"

"A single human brain can perceive pattern on the

scale of stars and galaxies," Tomiko said, "and interpret it as Love."

Mannon looked from one to the other of them; Harfex was silent.

"It'd be easier in the forest," Osden said. "Which of you will fly me over?"

"When?"

"Now. Before you all crack up or go violent."

"I will," Tomiko said.

"None of us will," Harfex said.

"I can't," Mannon said. "I… I'm too frightened. I'd crash the jet."

"Bring Eskwana along. If I can pull this off, he might serve as a medium."

"Are you accepting the Sensor's plan, Coordinator?" Harfex asked formally.

"Yes."

"I disapprove. I will come with you, however."

"I think we're compelled, Harfex," Tomiko said, looking at Osden's face, the ugly white mask transfigured, eager as a lover's face.

Olleroo and Jenny Chong, playing cards to keep their thoughts from their haunted beds, their mounting dread, chattered like scared children. "This thing, it's in the forest, it'll get you—"

"Scared of the dark?" Osden jeered.

"But look at Eskwana, and Porlock, and even Asnanifoil—"

"It can't hurt you. It's an impulse passing through

synapses, a wind passing through branches. It is only a nightmare."

They took off in a helijet, Eskwana curled up still sound asleep in the rear compartment, Tomiko piloting, Harfex and Osden silent, watching ahead for the dark line of forest across the vague gray miles of starlit plain.

They neared the black line, crossed it; now under them was darkness.

She sought a landing place, flying low, though she had to fight her frantic wish to fly high, to get out, get away. The huge vitality of the plant-world was far stronger here in the forest, and its panic beat in immense dark waves. There was a pale patch ahead, a bare knoll-top a little higher than the tallest of the black shapes around it; the not-trees; the rooted; the parts of the whole. She set the helijet down in the glade, a bad landing. Her hands on the stick were slippery as if she had rubbed them with cold soap.

About them now stood the forest, black in darkness. Tomiko cowered down and shut her eyes. Eskwana moaned in his sleep. Harfex's breath came short and loud, and he sat rigid, even when Osden reached across him and slid the door open.

Osden stood up; his back and bandaged head were just visible in the dim glow of the control-panel as he paused stooping in the doorway.

Tomiko was shaking. She could not raise her head. "No, no, no, no, no, no, no," she said in a whisper.

"No. No. No."

Osden moved suddenly and quietly, swinging out of the doorway, down into the dark. He was gone.

I am coming! said a great voice that made no sound. Tomiko screamed. Harfex coughed; he seemed to be trying to stand up, but did not do so.

Tomiko drew in upon herself, all centered in the blind eye in her belly, in the center of her being; and outside that there was nothing but the fear.

It ceased.

She raised her head; slowly unclenched her hands. She sat up straight. The night was dark, and stars shone over the forest. There was nothing else.

"Osden," she said, but her voice would not come.

She spoke again, louder, a lone bullfrog croak. There was no reply.

She began to realize that something had gone wrong with Harfex. She was trying to find his head in the darkness, for he had slipped down from the seat, when all at once, in the dead quiet, in the dark rear compartment of the craft, a voice spoke. "Good," it said.

It was Eskwana's voice. She snapped on the interior lights and saw the engineer lying curled up asleep, his hand half over his mouth.

The mouth opened and spoke. "All well," it said. "Osden—"

"All well," said the soft voice from Eskwana's mouth. "Where are you?" Silence.

"Come back."

Wind was rising. "I'll stay here," the soft voice said.

"You can't stay—"

Silence.

"You'd be alone, Osden!"

"Listen." The voice was fainter, slurred, as if lost in the sound of wind. "Listen. I will tell you well."

She called his name after that, but there was no answer. Eskwana lay still. Harfex lay stiller.

"Osden!" she cried, leaning out the doorway into the dark, wind-shaken silence of the forest of being. "I will come back. I must get Harfex to the base. I will come back, Osden!"

Silence and wind in leaves.

They finished the prescribed survey of World 4470, the eight of them; it took them forty-one days more. Asnanifoil and one or another of the women went into the forest daily at first, searching for Osden in the region around the bare knoll; though Tomiko was not in her heart sure which bare knoll they had landed on that night in the very heart and vortex of terror. They left piles of supplies for Osden, food enough for fifty years, clothing, tents, tools. They did not go on searching; there was no way to find a man alone, hiding, if he wanted to hide, in those unending labyrinths and dim corridors vine-entangled, root-floored. They might have passed within arm's reach of him and never seen him.

But he was there; for there was no fear any more. Rational, and valuing reason more highly after an intolerable experience of the immortal mindless,

Tomiko tried to understand rationally what Osden had done. But the words escaped her control. He had taken the fear into himself, and accepting had transcended it. He had given up his self to the alien, an unreserved surrender, that left no place for evil. He had learned the love of the Other, and thereby had been given his whole self. But this is not the vocabulary of reason.

The people of the Survey team walked under the trees, through the vast colonies of life, surrounded by a dreaming silence, a brooding calm that was half-aware of them and wholly indifferent to them. There were no hours. Distance was no matter. Had we but world enough and time... The planet turned between the sunlight and the great dark; winds of winter and summer blew fine, pale pollen across the quiet seas.

Gum returned after many surveys, years, and light-years, to what had several centuries ago been Smeming Port of Pesm. There were still men there to receive (incredulously) the team's reports and to record its losses: Biologist Harfex, dead of fear, and Sensor Osden, left as a colonist.

Maria Sibylla Merian, colored copper engraving from *Metamorphosis insectorum Surinamensium*, plate XLIII. "Spiders, ants and hummingbird on a branch of a guava" (Tarantula: Avicularia avicularia), 1705.

"9. This anecdote appears authentic because it has many Spinozan resonances. Spider-fights, or spider-fly fights, could have fascinated Spinoza for several reasons: 1. from the standpoint of the exteriority of necessary death; 2. from the standpoint of the composition of relations in nature (how the web expresses a relationship of the spider with the world, one which appropriates, as such, relations peculiar to the fly); 3. from the standpoint of the relativity of perfections (how a state that marks an imperfection of man, e.g., warfare, can on the contrary testify to a perfection if it is related to a different essence such as that of insects: cf. *Letter XIX* to Blyenbergh). We will encounter these problems again in a later chapter." [see pp.249]

AYESHA SIDDIQI

Response*

[...] SO FOR PLATFORMS like Tumblr, Face-book, Twitter, all of its users are the ones generating value for it, right? We're essentially running their product for them for free. And in doing so, certainly there are some obvious benefits, so you know we're in this moment that typically marginalized voices have greater access to the community and connectivity that we're here to discuss today. They can reach each other, I mean there's obvious gains to be had there, but we're also increasingly mistaking visibility for power.

And for these typically marginalized voices—and it's interesting, the people I've noticed at this point in time that have the most angst around the Internet or the social web, people who work in media and are like, "Oh, gosh, Internet is just the worst, right, Twitter is terrible." and of course all of these opinions are being voiced on the Internet and on Twitter. They're typically people that the rest of the world has been pretty kind to and the people that have almost the greatest investment in these spaces and spend a great deal of time on them are people that the rest of the world isn't that friendly to and it was initially space to escape the daily hostilities and aggressions and of course for people of color, people who aren't straight, queer, gay, LGBTQ communities. These are really vital developments. Our ability to produce and establish

---

*Transcript of response to 'Connectivity and Community' panel at *SuperScript* Conference, Walker Art Centre, 2015

community, our ability to connect, the way its been facilitated for the social web, has in fact changed many lives.

And one category I spend a lot of time thinking about is students of color who struggle with mental illness issues and the ways in which that mental health resources are either completely designed not to serve them, but actively reproduce colonial violence in the ways in which those administrators are trained to deal with students of color or cultural differences that they may encounter. And how so many young people had then turned to the social web to generate their own survival scripts to produce ways of coping with things like depression, anxiety, thoughts of self-harm, and that's a form of quote-unquote life hacking that I'm way more interested in than cutting up an old takeout container to make a plate. It's bizarre how what the word "life hacking" gets used to mean and its association with tech bros when there are people doing far more interesting and innovative work just for the pure pursuit of being able to move through the world with relative grips on their sanity and safety.

So while those communities are being developed and are being incredible resources and incredibly empowering, which I want to later distinguish from actual power, I absolutely recognize those benefits and boons and I'm happy for people who have access to these spaces and conversations and can more freely speak their truths and learn from each other.

This is relevant to anyone: from young people connecting over shared experiences on mental health communities, on Tumblr or other blogging platforms, or the fact that the establishment media is no longer shielded from the necessary and relevant critiques that people outside of it can offer and how so much of what's described as Twitter backlash is really the resistance to the historical and still currently ongoing erasure of voices and discourses and essentially colonial perspectives on culture writing. So I'm absolutely optimistic about what it means for media and publishing that a lot of typically marginalized voices are able to speak out and speak to establishment media and to each other and there's a great deal of power in the affirmations that that enables and allows.

While all of that is happening, all of the, the visibility that follows those critiques or the types of thinkers and writers that gain attention aren't—don't have then the access to actual capital versus the social capital that their visibility on social web may accrue for them, and it's also important to distinguish visibility from, you know, the fact that what it can oftentimes really produce is the same social—same vulnerabilities that their social position, the rest of the world had for them. So a lot of the writers of color, young thinkers, black women, trans individuals who are creating community, creating content, running Tumblr and Twitter for these corporations, they don't own what they're putting out there. They're entirely subject to the corporate ownership of those platforms, and they're also vulnerable to what that—to all of the harms that that visibility can bring them, whether it's routine harassment, a lot of, you know, what's called—what's attributed to Twitter or something unique to these individual platforms is really just the misogyny and racism that exists elsewhere anyway, and the way that those patterns of oppression replicate themselves, it's the same sense of entitlements to the ideas and labor and bodies and images of people of color and of women only now it's on these platforms instead.

And so there's the micro-level of individuals who are then subject to something that's as unfortunately routine as harassment, to being stalked online, from online to their real-world lives, having their addresses revealed and released, having their pictures taken and circulated without their consent. These patterns then also—and those vulnerabilities are also present for anyone trying to produce independent alternative projects, and what I'm seeing with the rise of a different form of digital DIY culture is the foreclosure of indie culture and that means that sure, it may seem exciting to have a website that you describe as a magazine, or to Kickstart a project or to, you know, connect potential audiences or consumers to the thing that you want to put out into the world, you don't—no longer need the same skillset, you don't need to be a coder, you don't need to be a manufacturer, you can just use the apps and websites that are now designed to do that for you, to fill those gaps, right?[...]

There's slightly different pattern of that same social control that happens on platforms like Twitter and Tumblr. These spaces were increasingly just shortening the gap between, you know, the cultural production of cool by the alternative, by the young, and its co-option by corporations, and essentially at ever-increasing rates, teaching corporations to be more efficient at advertising to us, because we're with our communities being so public, inviting them to take even more detailed essentially, you know, snapshots of the ways in which people are making their community and mimic those patterns in order to better advertise to us.

So you see that on Tumblr with promoted posts being designed to look like any other Tumblr post but they always inevitably stand out quite starkly because the language and image style that they're reliant on is one that was produced and people are familiar with because they made it themselves with references that are relevant to their own community and it's very, very obvious when someone who's not part of your community tries to do that, thinking of all the slang generated by you know, black teens on Vine that way, way later will eventually move to white and non-black communities and then a Denny's Twitter account telling you that their pancakes are on fleek.

So that cycle, which is not particularly new, in the history of the co-option of cool has become markedly accelerated and that co-option is not what's interesting. Advertisers being corny because they're a day late and a dollar short is only interesting because it's good for a laugh. What is interesting is that within the surveillance state, that acceleration reveals the relationship that these platforms, which we always forget are just actually corporations, are you know, mistaken for these bastions of democracy.

When the social web was first blowing up and places that couldn't really be described as digital natives, places like CNN and other media outlets were quickly trying to catch up investing so many resources and having, you know, robust online presence, and the subject of community engagement, you know, became an entire department that media outlets have, what is interesting about that is all of the voices that make these spaces vibrant and interesting and worth being on, because they're offering commentary you won't get elsewhere because they're breaking news on the ground, that other outlets are slowly struggling to get at.

At the end of the day, they're only more—they're only producing for free all of the methods that places that have always had money and always had reach and resources are able to use and I think this is more insidious than simple co-option because the Internet is supposed to be a force that's more democratic, supposed to be a force that produces more connectivity and community, who is it ultimately connecting?

And visibility in a surveillance state is not power, and all of the historical vulnerabilities that have existed for marginalized voices are simply migrating onto digital spaces and all of the exciting and vital work that people are doing to make their lives a little easier to bypass or life-hack all of the deficiencies in you know, their work-places or classrooms or day to day experiences by con-necting or communicating with each other exist in an ecosystem that's primed for their continued exploitation, that remains in many ways hostile to them, the misogyny that a female academic might encounter at a publication or within her department at school is easily replicated by misogyny you encounter in your Twitter mentions or in the comments section of something you write.

The entitlement to the emotional intellectual labor of people of color that exists in establishment media and academia is easily replicated by the entitlement exercised over these people's work online, and all of the places that we were meant to subvert by being online, by bypassing traditional, you know, paths that were barred from us by being able to avoid and then eventually make irrelevant gatekeepers to genres like cultural criticism, those gains have to be seen in light of the fact that all of this exciting interesting work, whether it's done, you know, whether it falls within the category of cultural criticism, or as I was referencing earlier, communities dedicated to helping each other live a little bit more honestly in their public realms, or connect over subjects that would be taboo in their day-to-day, you know, they—in the—you know, in the long game, these are communities that I'm still really concerned about. Because all of what can be seen as empowerment, people finally being able to speak and speak to each other and say what needs to be said, I think a lot of what's called empowerment on the Internet is referring to stories, sharing stories of their own lives and of each other's and being able to just simply speak. That has not, and I don't see it under existing conditions, translate to actual power. These are still interactions mediated by corporations. Those corporations and who runs them is still fundamentally the same as...you know it looks just like power has always looked in this country, very white, very male, and very removed from all of the communities and people, people of color, LGBTQ individuals that participate on these platforms, so as much as I've appreciated the past few years of all of the rest of us getting to speak and getting to be heard, which is a relatively recent and innovative and exciting development, we haven't reached power that is truly—that can truly compete with historical power structures.

And seeing the same patterns of erasure, violence, entitlement, that exist offline be easily adaptable and have evolved to online spaces and to see that these communities, whether it's someone bullied by members outside their communities, whether it's TCOT* activists trying to search your address and circulating your pictures because you're a Muslim that's going to bring down America, which is something that any Muslim who tweets online will hear at some point in their life, that's

*Top Conservatives on Twitter

something that we haven't yet found a way to evolve, and so all of the words that I found being used to describe this moment in time, and even use myself, things like this is empowering, this is exciting, the credit that these corporate platforms are given for revolutions like the Arab Spring or for movements like Black Lives Matter, that has to be reconciled eventually, or at least understood within the fact that ultimately these quote-unquote content creators, whether it's a makeup reviewer that you know has an audience of millions online or a Twitter user with thousands and thousand of followers and has huge reach, they don't own what they are putting out there, because we're all just running for free these platforms and these are at the end of the day corporations and I think the understanding of the social web as less an organic and natural digital space that we're all getting together and sort of holding hands around the fire which is kind of the sense for a lot typically marginalized communities, that you know that the communication and the word of the day, the community that these spaces have been able to generate, there's no ownership, there's only again, free labor, and for me, that's not new, and that's not encouraging. […]

Angels Rig Hook*

Where is my mind?

An abandoned oil rig stands in for the garden of
Eden. A garden is a walled space with vegetation.
It contains encrypted knowledge of good and evil.
777 terabytes of data contained in a single gram
of DNA. Wiping a tear off your cheek. *Salty.*

The ocean is grey. Makes you feel like there's
something wrong with it. What's the word?
'Contaminated'
Mandate Tonic,
Dance Titan Om,
An albatross has swallowed an Evian bottle.
When 2 become 1.

Like all people, they contained multitudes.
Like all situations, this was several situations at once.
Sometimes I looked away and ate peanuts and drank
Club Mate. Sometimes I thought about what time
it was. Then I was on the verge of tears.
Then I laughed a lot.

---

*Text by Jaakko Pallasvuo. Listen on soundcloud.

420 Park Avenue
Drexciya
François Rabelais
Quake 7 Arena
Caiman Nearness
Arcane Sans Mine
Amnesia Scanner

In a taxicraft. Magnetic hover. Tunnels. Plebs light
fires and roast stray cats. Taste memory of gnawing
on stringy cat meat. Cats are mostly bones and fur.
Memories of paper money, also on fire. Memories
of diamonds. Rare minerals, tea bowls repaired
with gold.
Kintsugi. Gnu I Kits. King Suit.
Nothing less than a 1000 years old.

Street view, upper level:
Gregorian monks in technical fabrics. Robes with
mesh and intelligence. uv face tattoos glow
in the dark. Yellow contacts, sharp fangs.
Monks are chanting:
Google Krishna,
Shrinkage Go Lo,
Angels Rig Hook,
Regal Kings ooh,

Ice cream melting on his chest.

Yourdicklooksgreatinthoseheels.com

Handguns, rare butterflies. elaborate prison tattoo
of a tiger in mid-leap.

Augmented reality contact lenses.

Red bull energy drink.

Fleshlight. S*hell* fight.

Septum streched, thicker rings are more beautiful.

Chain on neck.

Bull ring on nose.

F*ake* l*ashe*s. AFK l*ashe*s.

Nails so long that these hands can
        no longer grab things.

Voice control override.

This could be us but you playin'

thunderdome
thunderdome anagrams

We're gonna take everything before we secess.
We need more weapons. Hi-speed Wi-Fi provided
by drones is a given. *Arab money in ciphered curren-*
cies. Treasure island. Buccaneers and buried gold.

A stream of more or less violent crimes.
What was violence again?

Floor 312. We're there. I hand the driver a flake
of skin and a fingernail.

The oil rig. A bird flies over. *We extend our arm and*
stand completely still. Bird lands. Bird makes sound.
Gently touch bird. It lets that happen. Bird says:
_____ . *Identify bird: sparrow. Place*
filter on sparrow. Mosaic, turbulent displace, hue/
saturation. Bird is simplified, jagged edges,
orange for now.

scan

_____
____

Cosmos

Chapter 1

I'LL TELL YOU about another adventure that's even more strange . . .

Sweat, Fuks is walking, I'm behind him, pant legs, heels, sand, we're plodding on, plodding on, ruts, clods of dirt, glassy pebbles flashing, the glare, the heat humming, quivering, everything is black in the sunlight, cottages, fences, fields, woods, the road, this march, from where, what for, a lot could be said, actually I was worn out by my father and mother, by my family in general, I wanted to prepare for at least one of my exams and also to breathe in change, break loose, spend time someplace far away. I went to Zakopane, I'm walking along the Krupowki, thinking about finding a cheap little boarding house, when I run into Fuks, his faded-blond, carroty mug, bug-eyed, his gaze smeared with apathy, but he's glad, and I'm glad, how are you, what are you doing here, I'm looking for a room, me too, I have an address—he says—of a small country place where it's cheaper because it's far away, out in the sticks some-where. So we go on, pant legs, heels in the sand, the road and the heat, I look down, the earth and the sand, pebbles sparkling, one two, one two, pant legs, heels, sweat, eyelids heavy from a sleepless night on the train, nothing but a rank-and-file trudging along. He stopped.

WITOLD GOMBROWICZ

Cosmos

I

BUT LET ME TELL YOU about another, even
more curious adventure.

It was sweltering. Fuchs tramped on ahead and
I followed behind. Trouser-legs. Heels. Sand. On we
plodded. Earth. Ruts. The road was vile. Gleams from
shiny pebbles, the air shimmering and buzzing with heat,
everything black with sunlight. Houses, fences, fields
and woods. What a road. What a tramp. Where we were
coming from and why... but that would be a long story.
The fact of the matter was that I was sick of my parents,
and indeed the whole family, and also I wanted to pass
at least one exam and get right away from it all. So I took
off to Zakopane and was walking through Krupowki,
wondering where to find a good cheap pension, when
whom should I run into but Fuchs. Fuchs had carroty
hair, fading into blond, and dead, protruding, fishlike
eyes, but he was pleased to see me and I was pleased
to see him, how are you, what are you doing here, I'm
looking for a room, so am I, I've got an address (he said),
a little place right out in the country where it's cheaper
because it's a long way out, right outside the village.
So off we went. Trouser-legs, heels in the sand, the road,
the heat. I stared at my feet. Earth and sand, glistening
pebbles, one foot after the other, trouser-legs, heels,

"Let's rest."

"How far is it?"

"Not far."

I looked around and saw whatever there was to see, and it was precisely what I didn't want to see because I had seen it so many times before: pines and fences, firs and cottages, weeds and grass, a ditch, footpaths and cabbage patches, fields and a chimney... the air... all glistening in the sun, yet black, the blackness of trees, the grayness of the soil, the earthy green of plants, everything rather black. A dog barked, Fuks turned into a thicket.

"It's cooler here."

"Let's go on."

"Wait a minute. Let's sit down a while."

He ventured deeper into the bushes where recesses and hollows were opening up, darkened from above by a canopy of intertwining hazel branches and boughs of spruce, I ventured with my gaze into the disarray of leaves, twigs, blotches of light, thickets, recesses, thrusts, slants, bends, curves, devil knows what, into a mottled space that was charging and receding, first growing quiet, then, I don't know, swelling, displacing everything, opening wide... lost and drenched in sweat, I felt the sweat, my eyes kept blinking with fatigue, I had slept badly in the train, and on we plodded in the sweltering heat. There was nothing but this endless, ground-level plodding.

He stopped.

'Shall we stop and have a rest?'

'How far do we still have to go?'

'Not very far now'.

I looked round at what was to be seen, though I had no desire to see it, because I had seen it so often already—pines and hedges, firs and houses, grass and weeds, a ditch, footpaths and flower-beds, fields and a chimney. The air was shimmering with sunlight, but black, the trees were black, the earth was grey, the vegetation at ground-level was green, but everything was pretty black. A dog barked. Fuchs strode off towards a roadside thicket.

'It'll be cooler,' he said.

'No, let's go on.'

'Let's have a short rest first.'

He plunged deeper into the thicket, where there were shady nooks and corners under the mingling branches of hazel-trees and pines. I gazed into the maze of leaves and branches, dappled light, dense vegetation, gaps and recesses and windings and slopes and yawning chasms and heaven knows what else besides that advanced on us and receded, forced us aside and yielded to us, jostled us and made way for us… Lost and dripping with sweat, I felt the bare, black earth under my feet. But there, ground below, black and bare. There was something stuck between the trees— something was protruding that was different and strange, though indistinct… and this is what my companion was also watching.

"A sparrow." "Ah."

It was a sparrow. A sparrow hanging on a piece of wire. Hanged. Its little head to one side, its beak wide open. It was hanging on a thin wire hooked over a branch.

Remarkable. A hanged bird. A hanged sparrow. The eccentricity of it clamored with a loud voice and pointed to a human hand that had torn into the thicket— but who?

Who hanged it, why, for what reason?… my thoughts were entangled in this overgrowth abounding in a million combinations, the jolting train ride, the night filled with the rumble of the train, lack of sleep, the air, the sun, the march here with this Fuks, there was Jasia and my mother, the mess with the letter, the way I had "cold-shouldered" my father, there was Roman, and also Fuks's problem with his boss in the office (that he's been telling me about), ruts, clods of dirt, heels, pant legs, pebbles, leaves, all of it suddenly fell down before the bird, like a crowd on its knees, and the bird, the eccentric, seized the reign… and reigned in this nook.

"Who could have hanged it?"

"Some kid."

"No. It's too high up."

among the branches, was something peculiar and strange, though at first I could not make out exactly what it was. My companion had seen it and was staring at it too.

'It's a sparrow.'

'Good heavens alive.'

Yes, it was a sparrow. A sparrow hanging from a bit of wire. It had been hanged. Its little head was bent and its mouth wide open. It was hanging by a bit of wire attached to a branch of a tree.

Extraordinary. A hanged bird. A hanged sparrow. This shrieking eccentricity indicated that a human hand had penetrated this fastness. Who on earth could have done such a thing, and why? I wondered, standing in the midst of this chaos, this proliferating vegetation with its endless complications, my head full of the rattle and clatter of the nightlong train journey, insufficient sleep, the air and the sun and the tramp through the heat with this man Fuchs, and Jesia and my mother, the row about the letter and my rudeness to the old man, and Julius, and also Fuchs's troubles with his chief at the office (about which he had told me), and the bad road, and the ruts and lumps of earth and heels, trouser-legs, stones, and all this vegetation, all culminating like a crowd genuflecting before this hanged sparrow reigning triumphant and eccentric over this outlandish spot.

'Who on earth could have done a thing like that?'

"Some boy or other.'

'No, it's too high.'

"Let's go."

But he didn't stir. The sparrow was hanging. The ground was bare but in some places short, sparse grass was encroaching on it, many things lay about, a piece of bent sheet metal, a stick, another stick, some torn cardboard, a smaller stick, there was also a beetle, an ant, another ant, some unfamiliar bug, a wood chip, and so on and on, all the way to the scrub at the roots of the bushes—he watched as I did. "Let's go." But he went on standing, looking, the sparrow was hanging, I was standing, looking. "Let's go." "Let's go." But we didn't budge, perhaps because we had already stood here too long and the right moment for departure had passed… and now it was all becoming heavier, more awkward… the two of us with the hanging sparrow in the bushes… and something like a violation of balance, or tactlessness, an impropriety on our part loomed in my mind…
I was sleepy.

"Well, let's get going!" I said, and we left…
leaving the sparrow in the bushes, all alone.

Translated from the Polish by Danuta Borchardt.
Yale University Press, 2005.
(All orthography: [sic])

'Let's go.'

But he didn't budge. The sparrow went on hanging. Except for some grassy patches, the earth was bare. A lot of things were lying about: a strip of galvanised iron, a twig, another twig, a torn cardboard box, a broken off branch. There were also a beetle and an ant, and another ant, an unknown worm, a log, and so on and so forth, all the way to the undergrowth at the foot of the trees. He stared at all this, just as I did. 'Let's go,' he said, but he stayed where he was and went on staring, and the sparrow went on hanging, and I stayed there and went on staring too. 'Come on,' he said, but we didn't move, perhaps because we had already stayed there too long and had missed the right moment for going, and now, with that sparrow hanging in the trees, the situation grew graver and more unmanageable every moment, and I had the feeling that there was something disproportionate, untactful or unmannerly about us. I was sleepy.

'Come on,' I said, and off we went, leaving the sparrow in the trees behind us, alone.

Translated Eric Mosbacher and Alastair Hamilton.
Grove Press, 1967.
(All orthography: [sic])

P. 19 – 20

In 1962 and 1963, Robert Glasse and I presented evidence gathered in two extended stays among the Fore that kuru had spread through the Fore population in recent times, and that its high incidence in the early 1960s was related to the cannibal consumption of deceased kuru victims... Our cannibalism hypothesis seemed to fit the epidemiological evidence. The first Australian government patrols in the late 1940s reported cannibalism throughout the entire kuru region. By 1951, the Berndts, living on the North Fore borders, noted that government intervention had put a stop to cannibalism in that area, although it was still practiced surreptitiously farther afield... Thus, in the South Fore, the area with the highest incidence of kuru, cannibalism had continued later than in the North.

P. 175

Significantly, not all Fore were cannibals. Some elderly men rarely ate human flesh, and small children residing with their mothers ate what their mothers gave them. Initiated [male] youths, at approximately age ten, moved to the men's house, away from their mothers, where they began to observe the cultural practices and dietary taboos that define masculinity. Consuming the dead was appropriate for adult women but not men, who feared the pollution and physical depletion associated with eating a corpse. The early medical reports, indicating that kuru occurred among women, children of both sexes, and a few elderly men, thus matched Fore rules of cannibal consumption.

P. 20

...Men in this protein-scarce society claimed the preferred form of protein (wild boar, domestic pigs), whereas women supplemented their lesser allotment of pork with small game, insects, frogs, and dead humans.

IAN MCCAMMON

Evidence of Heuristic Traps in Recreational Avalanche Accidents

[...] **WHEN MOST OF US THINK** of decision making, we imagine a process where we review relevant information, weigh alternatives, then decide. There's no doubt that we are capable of making some decisions this way, but the method requires time and mental energy— resources that are in short supply in a busy and complex world. In a typical day we make hundreds of decisions, both large and small, and we must make them efficiently.

To balance our constant need to make good decisions against our need to make them quickly, we often use simple rules of thumb, or heuristics. Heuristics give quick results because they rely on only one or two key pieces of evidence, and though they are not always right they work often enough to guide us through routine but complex tasks such as driving or shopping (cit.). Because we use them so often, heuristics tend to operate at the threshold of our consciousness, a fact that has been relentlessly exploited by countless advertising and marketing campaigns (cit.).

In order for heuristic decision making to work in high-risk situations, the cues we rely on must be relevant to the actual hazard. If, out of unconscious habit, we choose the wrong cues our decisions can be catastrophically wrong. This mismatch, where we base decisions on familiar but inappropriate cues, is known as a heuristic trap. [...] In this paper, I present evidence that four heuristic traps—familiarity, social proof, commitment and scarcity—have played key roles in recreational avalanche accidents. For each trap, I examine its statistical significance, the influences of group size and level of avalanche training, and how reliable or unreliable the underlying heuristic might be for making decisions in avalanche terrain. Data for this study came from accident records maintained by the Colorado Avalanche Information Center, published accounts in *The Snowy Torrents* (cit.), and various internet and newspaper resources. Over the course of the study, I reviewed 622 recreational avalanche incidents involving 1180 individuals in the United States between 1972 and 2001. [...]

3.2 The familiarity heuristic

The familiarity heuristic is the tendency to believe that our behavior is correct to the extent that we have done it before. In essence, this heuristic amounts to a kind of mental habit where our past actions are proof that a particular behavior is appropriate. For example, when we drive to work each day, we generally don't review the pros and cons of all possible routes; we simply take the most familiar one.

Credo

THE BUSH IS NEUTRAL. It is neither for nor against me. My comfort depends on what I can do for myself and how much I know about using the bush materials around me.

Becoming angry, depressed or unhappy does little to help me in my situation. I will try to think positive thoughts and find ways to be thankful for what I have. When I am not sure of what to do I will stop, relax and think out the situation before I act.

I realize moving about when I do not know where I am or where I am going will make it more difficult for others to find me.

My concern at this moment is to make myself comfortable for tonight. I shall shelter myself from wind, rain or snow and build a fire to warm up.

I will not let fear or panic rule my mind as this only works against me. The bush is inert. It is incapable of doing me harm.

Equipped To Survive® Presents
The Survival Forum™

Please review The Survival Forum Rules and Courtesies.
You are not logged in. [Log In]
ETS Forums » Forums » The Survival Forum » The Survival Forum »

The " bush" is not inert or neutral

Page 1 of 3   1 2 3 >

Topic Options [print topic/ switch to threaded mode]

The familiarity heuristic is especially powerful because it is simple and it frees us from having to go through the same time-consuming decision processes again and again, only to arrive at what is usually the same conclusion. People unconsciously use this heuristic dozens of times each day, so it's no surprise that it is routinely exploited in the advertising and retail industries (cit.).

To evaluate the possible influence of the familiarity heuristic in avalanche accidents, I rated each group's familiarity with the accident site where their familiarity was reported (377 cases). Most accidents (69%) occurred on slopes that were very familiar to the victims. Fewer accidents occurred on slopes that were somewhat familiar (13%) and unfamiliar (18%) to the victim. In the subsequent analysis, I made comparisons only between the "very familiar" and "unfamiliar" categories. [...]

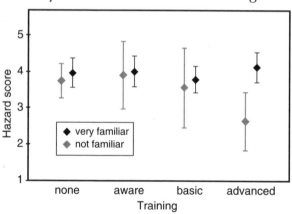

Fig. 1. Comparison of hazard scores by training in familiar and unfamiliar terrain, showing the 95% confidence interval about each mean.

The "bush" is not inert or neutral   #141147 - 07/24/08 11:39 AM

dweste 😐

Pooh-Bah

Registered: 02/16/08

Posts: 2463

Loc: Central California

Hacksaw had been using a signature quote from Mors Kochanski to the effect that the bush is inert.

BruceZed posted: "Not to digress to much but in my opinion the bush is not really inert, it is neutral when it come to whether we are going to live or die during a survival situation."

I invited both of them to make this idea a new topic.

Seeing no new topic posted, I started this thread.

I do not believe any natural environment is either inert or neutral. A Coast Guard search and rescue diver put it well: "The ocean is trying to kill you."

I think the same is true everywhere in the outdoors whether on land or sea: nature wants to digest you. Unless you act to prevent it, the nutrients in your body will be lost to nature.

It starts with either heat loss or dehydration, and goes on to direct attack by creatures large and small. Even the part of nature represented by your own body demands water, food, shelter, etc.

Inert? Neutral? I don't think so.

What do you think?

Thanks.

Top

#141148 - 07/24/08 12:01 PM Re: The " bush " is not inert or neutral [Re: dweste]

bsmith 😐

day hiker

Addict

Registered: 02/15/07

Posts: 576

Loc: ventura county, ca

i too have questioned - in my mind - that signature.

i assume - always a bad move - that 'bush' means nature or the whole outdoors.

merriam's dictionary defines inert:

The lowest levels of avalanche training showed no sensitivity to familiarity cues. This result is reasonable since untrained victims lacked the knowledge to reduce their exposure to avalanche hazard, regardless of whether they were in familiar or unfamiliar terrain. At the highest level of training, familiarity with the slope corresponded to a significant increase in hazard score. At the 95% confidence level, hazard score increased by 1.5±0.8 hazard indicators (Fig. 3). In unfamiliar terrain, people with advanced avalanche knowledge appeared to use their risk-reduction skills to their advantage. But in familiar terrain, these groups exposed themselves to the same level of hazard as other groups with less or no training (p_{KW} = 0.76 for all groups in familiar terrain). It thus appears that, in victims with advanced training, familiarity with a slope tended to negate the benefits of knowledge and experience.

The familiarity heuristic is fairly reliable in everyday decisions, but how well does it work in avalanche terrain? We can make a preliminary estimate from some simple observations. First, most accidents happen on slopes that are familiar to the victims. While it's likely that people tend to recreate more often on slopes they are familiar with, the high percentage of accidents on familiar slopes suggests that familiarity alone does not correspond to a substantially lower incidence of triggering an avalanche. Second, a comparison of familiarity cues with the posted avalanche hazard shows no preference among avalanche victims for familiar slopes during times of

1: lacking the power to move

well, nature grows and while growing, moves. now
of course nature doesn't move to cincinnati. but nature
does overgrow anything in its path - see mayan or cam-
bodian temples.

2: very slow to move or act : sluggish

now this fits nature.

3: deficient in active properties; especially : lacking a
usual or anticipated chemical or biological action.

nature very much has a 'usual or anticipated chemical or
biological action.' in many cases, extremely predictable.

so, in my mind, by definition, inert is a mixed bag. but i
think it is incorrect.

now if he's trying to say that nature has no emotion and
has no interest in any anticipated outcome, i would
agree with that.

in my mind, nature - the bush - is what it is. it is not
positive, it is not negative, it just is.

pretty heavy stuff for so early in the morning.

Edited by bsmith (07/24/08 12:48 PM)

"Everyone should have a horse. It is a great way to store meat without refriger-
ation. Just don't ever get on one." - ponder's dad

Top
#141152 - 07/24/08 12:17 PM Re: The " bush" is not inert or neutral
[Re: bsmith]
unimogbert 😊   I too have looked at that signature and dismissed it as
Old Hand   simply wrong.

Registered: 08/10/06   The saying that the NPS puts up on trail info signs I
Posts: 837   think expresses it better. "The mountains don't care."
Loc: Colorado   And that's nature at it's most benign.

lower hazard (p_{KW} = 0.55). In other words, it appears unlikely that the familiarity heuristic is linked to some third factor that substantially reduces avalanching. [...]

3.3 The social proof heuristic

The social proof heuristic is the tendency to believe that a behavior is correct to the extent that other people are engaged in it. Cialdini (cit.) provides a comprehensive review of research supporting the idea that others' behavior and even mere presence has a powerful influence on our decisions. In general, we rely on the social proof heuristic most when we are uncertain and when others similar to ourselves are engaged in an activity. Tremper (cit.) considers this heuristic to be one of the major causes of avalanche accidents.

To evaluate the possible influence of the social proof heuristic in avalanche accidents, I compared the hazard scores of accidents where the victims had met others similar to themselves to the hazard scores of accidents where the victim(s) had met no one. The difference between these two conditions is significant; victims that had met similar others prior to the accident exposed their group to more hazard factors than groups that had met no one.

[...] The largest increases in hazard exposure with social proof cues appeared in groups with basic and advanced avalanche training (Fig. 4). For these victims, the mere presence of people outside the victims' group correlated with a significant increase in exposure to

In reality, there are elements (insects, reptiles, arachnids, and mammals) out there that are trying to eat your lunch, or eat YOU for lunch. They are actively seeking your demise or just wanting to abuse you for their survival benefit. It's without malice but it's active.

So you could expand the topic considerably.
The mountains don't care if you aren't having a good time.
The mountains don't care if you think they are beautiful.
The mountains don't care if you die here.
The mountains don't care if you are injured here and die somewhere else.
The mountains don't care if your wife never sees you alive again.
The mountains don't care if you have to cut off your arm to save your life.
The mountains don't care if you fall thru the ice and die of hypothermia.
The mountains don't care if that rattlesnake never gets to consume you as prey. (Some other creatures will though.)

etc.

I suppose you could also find an analogue in daily life.
The other driver doesn't care.
The cop doesn't care.
The guy who designed this highway doesn't care :-)

Top
#141153 - 07/24/08 12:31 PM Re: The " bush" is not inert or neutral
[Re: dweste]
Russ 😊
Carpal Tunnel

Registered: 06/02/06
Posts: 4436
Loc: SOCAL

Inert is not a good term to describe nature because it implies that nature is powerless. However, a good argument could be made for neutral.

Nature in general doesn't care whether you live or die. It can and has provided for our well being if/when we have known enough to take what we need. OTOH, nature won't give us this bounty on a silver platter, we have to take it and keep it and we may need to compete with other inhabitants of nature who are better suited.

Just as we can consider a salmon we catch in a stream to be part of what nature provides, the grizzly who's food we just

avalanche hazard. As with familiarity, this increase was easily sufficient to negate the risk-reduction benefits of avalanche training.

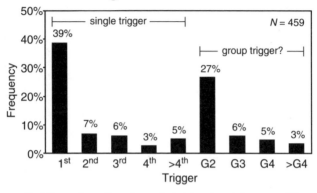

Fig 4. Comparison of hazard scores by training when victims met or did not meet other people prior to the accident, showing the 95% confidence interval about each mean.

If the social proof heuristic did in fact influence the victims' behavior in these accidents, its effect appears to be quite pronounced, particularly in victims with avalanche training. But is the heuristic reliable enough in avalanche terrain to justify such a high level of influence? One possible answer comes from examining one of the assumptions that underlies the social proof heuristic: the belief that a slope which has been skied/boarded/high marked is less likely to avalanche.

To explore how social proof cues relate to the stability of avalanche slopes, I examined how each avalanche was triggered. In the majority of cases, a single individual clearly triggered the slab but in 21% of the cases that person was not the first one on the slope. In the

took is also part of nature. Nature "in general" doesn't care whether the bear gets the salmon, we get the salmon or the bear gets us. Neutral is a good term.

Top

#141154 - 07/24/08 12:43 PM Re: The " bush" is not inert or neutral [Re: Russ]

Hacksaw

Unregistered

I'm not going to debate this one because Mors Kochanski is somebody who I really respect and admire...and he's a fellow Albertan!

The quote comes from his 'credo' which I'll quote here. I've done so without permission and have no affiliation with Mors or his school.

The bush is neutral. Is is neither for nor against me. My comfort depends on what I can do for myself and how much I know about using the bush materials around me. Becoming angry, depressed or unhappy does little to help me in my situation. I will try to think positive thoughts and find ways to be thankful for what I have. When I am not sure of what to do I will stop, relax, and think out the situation before I act.

I realize moving about when I do not know where I am or where I am going will make it difficult for others to find me.

My concern at this moment is to make myself comfortable for tonight. I shall shelter myself from wind, rain or snow and build a fire to warm up.

I will not let fear or panic rule my mind as this only works against me. The bush is inert. It is incapable off doing me harm.

Top

#141156 - 07/24/08 12:48 PM Re: The " bush" is not inert or neutral [Re: Russ]

BillLiptak

Enthusiast

Registered: 12/19/07
Posts: 259

Nature is a cruel mistess,just like I like 'em ;-) It kinda reminds me of an old song by Twisted Sister..... What you don't know can hurt you. Nature is all about change and balance. She will try to absorb you even as she provides for you.

-Bill Liptak

remainder of the cases there was more than one person on the slab when it fractured, so the exact trigger was unclear. In some cases, most notably those involving snowmobiles engaged in high marking, the slope had been heavily tracked prior to avalanching. One surprising result was that in 204 cases, the slope that avalanched either had tracks on it or there were tracks nearby.[...]

3.4 The commitment heuristic

The commitment heuristic is the tendency to believe that a behavior is correct to the extent that it is consistent with a prior commitment we have made. This heuristic is deeply rooted in our desire to be and appear consistent with our words, beliefs, attitudes and deeds (cit.). Public image aside, the heuristic works because it provides us a shortcut through complexity. Rather than sift through all the relevant information with each new development, we merely make a decision that is consistent with an earlier one. Given the ubiquity (many say the necessity) of the commitment heuristic in modern life, it's no surprise that our unconscious reliance on it frequently makes us unwitting shills in countless retail, charity and political campaigns (cit.).

To evaluate the possible influence of the commitment heuristic in avalanche accidents, I assigned each accident to one of three categories of commitment. Groups assigned to the high commitment category had a stated goal they were actively pursuing or a goal they were motivated to achieve because of approaching darkness, timing

Top

#141157 - 07/24/08 12:49 PM Re: The " bush" is not inert or neutral
[Re:]

Russ 😊   Originally Posted By: Hacksaw
Carpal Tunnel   . . .*The bush is inert. It is incapable off
                                 doing me harm.*

Registered: 06/02/06
Posts: 4436   How is he defining "bush"? That last line seems more
Loc: SOCAL   like someone convincing himself it's safe to go to sleep.
                                 Too bad Mors isn't here to explain the context of that
                                 statement.

Top

#141175 - 07/24/08 02:08 PM Re: The " bush" is not inert or neutral
[Re:]
unimogbert 😊

Old Hand   If he'd left off those last 2 sentences it would be a great
                                 statement.

Registered: 08/10/06
Posts: 837
Loc: Colorado

Top

#141179 - 07/24/08 02:37 PM Re: The " bush" is not inert or neutral
[Re: unimogbert]

Henry_Porter 😊   I always thought that signature was a comment on U.S.
Member   politics....

Registered: 03/24/07   Seriously, this is a very thought-provoking and practical
Posts: 111   topic. My interest and activities to be better equipped
                                 were started by the realization ("awakening" might be an
                                 even better word) that the world, people, life, God don't
                                 owe me ease and comfort and, as others have noted
                                 here, the natural world is indifference in general and
                                 many times hostile in particular to not only my ease but
                                 my life.

                                 Don't ask me how much of my life was spent under the
                                 delusion that the world, nature, society, government
                                 owed me ease and plenty. I'm glad for this forum.

Category	N_p	N_a	test	p
all accidents:	216	110	t	**0.022**
group size:				
1	30	11	t	0.83
2	63	37	t	0.98
3	44	29	t	0.13
4	31	12	t	0.64
>4	insufficient data		-	-
training:				
all levels	100	100	*ANOVA*	**0.043**

Table 3. Comparison between accidents where commitment cues were present (p) and absent (a). Significant differences exist between training levels.

or other constraints. Victims I assigned to the low commitment category did not appear motivated to achieve a specific goal, while victims I assigned to the no commitment category had unintentionally exposed themselves to avalanche hazard while engaged in non-goal oriented activity (wandering onto a cornice while the rest of the party was eating lunch, for example). This last group was not included in the analysis due to its small sample size (N = 13).

As shown in Table 3, the presence of commitment cues (high commitment) was significant over all groups.

3.5 The scarcity heuristic

Most skiers are familiar with the "powder fever" that seizes the public after a long-awaited snowstorm. Intent on getting first tracks down a favorite run, hordes of skiers flock to the lifts and the backcountry, often throwing caution to the wind as they compete with each other to consume the powder that is untracked for a limited time only. While this phenomenon is largely fueled by people's enjoyment of powder skiing, it probably has deeper roots in our attitudes about personal freedom.

A substantial body of research suggests that people react strongly, at times even aggressively, to any perceived restrictions to prerogatives they feel they are entitled to, regardless of whether or not they intend to exercise those prerogatives (cit.). This principle, called psychological reactance, emerges at about the age of two and pervades the fabric of our social environment. In our everyday decision making, psychological reactance manifests itself as the scarcity heuristic: we tend to distort the value of opportunities we perceive as limited and to compete with others to obtain them.

HAUDENOSAUNEE

PASSPORT

AUDRA SIMPSON

Mohawk Interruptus

WHAT DOES IT MEAN to be unrecognized?
What does it mean to not know what this means?
These are fundamentally political questions, and
thus require that I ask what it means to be recognized.
Political recognition is, in its simplest terms, to be seen
by another *as one wants to be seen*. Yet this regard is
not merely for the sanctity of the self; it is to appear
politically in formal and official forms, to have rights
that protect you from harm, that provide you access
to resources, or that protect certain resources. Patchen
Markell describes this succinctly as, in its base form,
"who we take ourselves and others to be" (cit.). One
might specify this as "to have rights, to have an effectual
capacity within a regime of power," as one should.
This then means to have the recognition of the state
and to have a passport that allows you as a formal
member of the community to move, to travel, to receive,
and exercise protections from harm. To be misrecog-
nized, Markell also helpfully states in his discussion
of the literature, is cast as a miscarriage of justice,
a "failure whether out of malice or ignorance, to extend
people the respect or esteem that is due to them in virtue
of who they are" (cit.). To then be unrecognized would
mean literally to be free from recognition and thus operate as a free-floating signifier, with politically unformed

from *Mohawk Interruptus: Political Life Across the Borders of Settler States*, Duke
University Press, Durham, 2014.

201

or unprotected identities—most important, as identities that are vulnerable to harm.[31] Here I want to argue that it is impossible to be free from an authorizing context, which means one is a slave, in some readings of Friedrich Hegel, and remains so until recognized in a system of mutuality ("I see you; you see me; this is reciprocal; this reciprocity signals justice"). We might, however, want to test this reading further through empiricism. Indigeneity and its imbrication with settler colonialism question the conditions of seeing (perhaps of writing) that are laid out in the master-bondsman allegory; this allows us to consider another vantage point in another perceptual and argumentative theatre or space of recognition. Settler colonialism structures justice and injustice in particular ways, not through the conferral of recognition of the enslaved but by the conferral of disappearance in subject. This is *not seeing* that is so profound that mutuality cannot be achieved. "Recognition" in either a cognitive or juridical sense is impossible. It simply would require too much contortion from one protagonist and not the other to be considered just.

In order to further our understanding of the Iroquois case, I want to move the discussion to the theatre of apprehension—the way in which we see and understand

31. The literature on political recognition is concerned largely with identities and state power. This literature does not deviate from the axis of the state even though the impetus for recognition itself is, in Hegelian terms, between two, unequal people (master and bondsman). Patchen Markell has described the translation of this issue into the terms of justice as a "thick form of respect" (2003, 7).

this scene of "recognition" / "nonrecognition"—into
the materiality of current settler nation-states. This is
a theatre that is more than a neutral and performative
dramaturgy; it is in fact a settler-colonial nation-state
with particular optics, expectations, and possibilities
for interpretation. Hegel's is a concern with the *position*
of the slave, not the slave himself; that subjectivity is
taken up by others. Frantz Fanon most forcefully argues
in *Black Skin: White Masks* that the slave is the black
man, and in this subjectifying allegory the black man
comprehends the scene as one of objectification, and in
this, the feeling of subjugation and the deep knowledge
of its context. The black man sees an economy that is
predicated upon the extraction of labor from specified
bodies in order to annex territories and fuel the accumulation of surplus.[32] Recognition, in this reading of
Hegel, is the basis for self-consciousness, and here taken
to be a political self-consciousness that will translate
into a revolutionary argument, a movement to un-
shackle oneself from this formula for self-perception.
Glen Coulthard[33] takes from Fanon's reading of Hegel

---

32. Fanon is reading the slave's apprehension of a global economy structured on the
extraction of his labor through absolute force, through nonconsent. My argument is
indebted to Glen Coulthard's reading of these texts in his article "Subjects of Empire"
(2007).

33. Coulthard takes this from Fanon's story of a white girl who sees him on the street
and says, "Mama, see the Negro! I'm frightened, frightened!" This is a scene of recognition that Fanon (writing as himself) relays and a gaze within that he " turn[ed] away"
from (Fanon [1967] in Coulthard 2007, 444, 54–6). This was an intense moment of
object formation (subject as object) that could have been potentially devastating in its
diminishment, but it was not; it became an occasion to move outside of the politics of
recognition into self-authorization and subject formation, again, by " turning away"
from the demeaning little girl and " inward and away from the master" (ibid.).

the impetus to "turn away" from the oppressor, to avert one's gaze and refuse the recognition itself.[34]

This moment of turning away can turn us toward Haudenosaunee assertions, which in different ways tell a story about a territory of willingness, a willingness to "stay enslaved." We could see this as a political strategy that is cognizant of an unequal relationship, understands the terms of bondage, and chooses to stay within them in order to assert a greater principle: nationhood, sovereignty, jurisdiction by those who are deemed to *lack* that power, a power that is rooted in historical precedent but is conveniently forgotten or legislated away. (cit.) Perhaps here we see a willingness to assert a greater principle and, in the assertion of this principle, to assert and be free whether this is apprehended as such or not. So in the Haudenosaunee political context it can mean recognition by another authoritative nexus (one's own?) and thereby call the other's into question. This negates the authority of the other's gaze.

---

34. See the analysis by Alyosha Goldstein (2008) of the legally and temporally based notion of "laches" (legally defined as a " reasonable amount of time") as operationalized by Supreme Court justice Ruth Bader Ginsburg in her decision on Oneida land claims in what is now New York State. For an argument regarding its nonprecedential nature and danger to Indigenous treaty claims, see Kathryn Fort 2009. I am grateful to P.J. Herne for calling this article to my attention.

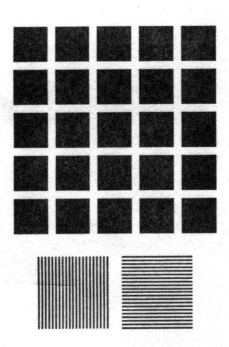

BLACK-EYED SUSAN
or
HOW PRINTS LOOK

ZOE TODD

From Fish Lives to Fish Law

The necessity of respecting game is still widely acknowledged by Inuit.
The awareness, that the continuity of society depends on the maintenance
of correct relationships with animals and the land, is still very strong.
(Aupilaarjuk et al. 1999: 2)

IN 2012, I SPENT EIGHT MONTHS living
and working in the Inuvialuit hamlet of Paulatuuq,
which is situated on the coast of the Beaufort Sea in
the Inuvialuit Settlement Region, in Canada's Northwest
Territories. I was interested in people's relationships to
fish, and how fishing relationships were being asserted
within the community in the face of cumulative colonial
and environmental impacts, including looming mining
interests, affecting the region. My first two degrees are
in Biology and Rural Sociology and when I started
ethnographic work in Paulatuuq, I still saw the relationships between humans and their environments with
colonial eyes: fish were food, fish were specimens, fish
were inputs in surveys and dry policy documents.

I knew better than to see fish this way. I grew up
fishing with my parents and sisters on Baptiste Lake
in north-central Alberta through the 1980s and 1990s.
I swam with the fish in that green prairie kettle lake every
summer throughout my entire childhood. I dreamt about
fish and their fish-lives beneath the inscrutable, rippled
lake-surface. I squealed with joy at the silver flash of
minnows in the shallows on lazy July days and, for many

dinners through my adolescence, we ate fish my step-dad caught in the Red Deer River, Pepper's Lake, and on his own re-watered wetland in central Alberta. But even with fish woven so intimately into every part of my life, it had never occurred to me that fish were also citizens, inter-locutors, story-tellers, and beings to whom I owed recip-rocal legal-governance and social duties. These lessons had been deeply erased from dominant (non-Indige-nous) public discourse in Alberta and I had not recog-nized the implicit ways fish were woven into my own life as more than food. This is the thing about colonization: it tries to erase the relationships and reciprocal duties we share across boundaries, across stories, across species, across space, and it inserts new logics, new principles, and new ideologies in their place.

Anishinaabe legal scholar John Borrows (cit.) argues that Canada is enlivened by legal pluralities. By this, he means that Canada is not governed only by laws derived from French and English legal systems, but that the coun-try is deeply shaped by the legal orders of First Peoples in North America whose territories were dispossessed by the colonizers. But through colonial sleight of hand, the Canadian State has tried to get us to forget that fish, too, are citizens within the territories we inhabit, that we share treaties and governance relationships with fish, plants, and other more-than-human agents.[1] Colonialism has worked tirelessly to erase the Indigenous

---

1. Vanessa Watts (2013:23) argues that: "habitats and ecosystems are better understood as societies from an Indigenous point of view; meaning that they have ethical structures, inter-species treaties and agreements, and further their ability to interpret, understand and implement. Non-human beings are active members of society. Not only are they active, they also directly influence how humans organize themselves into that society."

laws that govern Indigenous territories across Canada. This erasure obscures Indigenous legal orders and thinking in which humans, animals, water and land are integrated into nuanced and duty-full relationships with one another[2], replacing these legal-governance realities with ones that draw solely on anthropocentric French and English legal paradigms.

Whitefish (humpback whitefish—pikuktuuq)

Part of the struggle in identifying Indigenous law owes to their *implicit* nature, as Indigenous legal scholar Val Napoleon (cit.) points out:

> [M]any Indigenous peoples are not aware of the law they know—they just take it for granted and act on their legal obligations without talking about it. This is in contrast to explicit law, in which everything is explained and talked about and written down. Sometimes Indigenous peoples think that their laws have to look like western laws and so they try to describe them in western terms.

2. There is a rich literature on Indigenous legal orders and Indigenous cosmologies. I suggest reading the work of Mario Aupilarkuuk et al. (1999); John Borrows, Sarah Hunt, Kahente Horn-Miller, Sylvia McAdam, Val Napoleon, Tracey Lindberg, Jim Tully, Sharon Venne, Vanessa Watts and others.

It took me nearly my entire lifetime as a Red River Métis (otipemisiw, Michif) woman to learn to see the implicit Indigenous laws operating all around me throughout Indigenous territories in Canada. It was the experience of doing ethnography in Paulatuuq that taught me, finally, of the urgency and necessity of honouring Indigenous laws and the beautiful ways that they incorporate the more-than-human into legal-governance paradigms and discourses. In my work, I went looking for human responses to colonial relations, but quickly learned that resistance to colonial dispossession is articulated and mobilized not only through *human* means, but also through the bones, bodies, and movement of fish.

LAKE TROUT (anaaktiq)

In addition to focusing on the relation between fish, people, law, and colonialism my work also dwells on the complexities and paradoxes of doing ethnographic work as a Métis woman within the homeland of another

Indigenous people.[3] The greatest challenge I face in 'doing ethnography' is in becoming familiar and contending with tensions between, first, my obligations to Euro-Western academic research structures, paradigms, and ideals and, second, those duties I am bound to across, within, and between Indigenous legal orders and philosophies in Canada. In this tension lies the underlying reality that before I am a researcher or philosopher or academic, I am a citizen living within a complex, if at times unspoken, plurality of legal-governance systems—and inter-related histories, philosophies, stories, and ideas—operating in Canada. I draw my understanding of simultaneous interrelatedness and difference across settler-colonial and Indigenous thinking, stories, and laws from the work of Papaschase Cree Scholar Dwayne Donald (cit.), who outlines a principle of 'ethical relationality' as

> An ecological understanding of human relationality that does not deny difference, but rather seeks to more deeply understand how our different histories and experiences position us in relation to each other. This form of relationality is ethical because it does not overlook or invisibilize the particular historical, cultural, and social contexts from which a particular person understands and experiences living in the world. It puts these considerations at the forefront of engagements across frontiers of difference.

Ethical relationality encourages me to contend with my research relationships differently than the Canadian and British academies where I was trained. The University,

---

3. This is a tension that Indigenous scholars Olga Ulturgasheva and Stacy Rasmus (2014) interrogate in their ethnographic work across and between territories in Alaska and Siberia.

as a structure and a system, is built upon and informed by the laws and ethics of Euro-Western thinking and governance; it also operates to reify laws that are used to dispossess Indigenous peoples. However, to work in Indigenous territories and with Indigenous peoples' cosmologies in North America necessarily brings me into legal-governance and ethical relations across the plurality of laws that enliven these dynamic territories.

Donald's work invites us to attend to the space between and across a) the Euro-Western legal-ethical paradigms that build and maintain the academy-as-fort (or colonial outpost)[4], fixing it within imaginaries[5] of land as property and data as financial/intellectual transaction, and b) Indigenous legal orders and philosophies which enmesh us in *living* and *ongoing* relationships to one another, to land, to the more-than-human, and which fundamentally challenge the authority of Euro-Western academies which operate within unceded, unsurrendered and *sentient* lands and Indigenous territories in North America. It also brings our anthropological attention to the simultaneous and often contradictory negotiations that Indigenous peoples make across *both* sameness and difference in contending with the colonial Nation State in Canada.

---

4. Donald (2009: 4) interrogates the 'frontier logics' that still operate within Canada to separate Indigenous and non-Indigenous pedagogies and stories, and he employs the Fort as metaphor to illustrate the active way the education system works to keep Indigenous stories and philosophies outside the classroom.

5. In a recent talk in Ottawa, Canada in October 2015, Tracey Lindberg called these the 'colonial legal fictions' that the Canadian State relies upon to dispossess Indigenous peoples from living, thinking, and sentient lands.

211

In Paulatuuq, interlocutors Andy Thrasher, Millie Thrasher, Annie Illasiak and Edward and Mabel Ruben taught me that fish are more than food. Fish are simultaneously many things: food; sentient beings with whom humans share territory; specimens of study and regulation in wildlife co-management regimes; citizens and agents in legal-governance relationships, examples of what Ann Fienup-Riordan (cit.) calls 'active sites of engagement'. Across these sites, human-fish relations inform and capture memory, stories, teaching, and philosophies. I also learned that human-fish relations can act as 'micro-sites' across which fish and people, together, actively resist and shape colonial logics and processes within Inuvialuit territories. Just as humans can shape and experience the colonial encounter, so too can animals. Human-fish relations in Paulatuuq therefore present a plurality of meanings, strategies and principles for those enmeshed within them. As a result, fish pluralities in Paulatuuq deeply inform a vibrant and creative set of local strategies through which some community members have refracted colonial State formations of human-animal and human-environmental relations (cit.).

Annie Illasiak, an elder I worked with in Paulatuuq, repeated the same lesson to me several times while I was working and living in the community. That teaching was 'you never go hungry in the land if you have fish'[6]. At first, I thought she meant this teaching as a purely utilitarian subsistence or survival lesson: even if every other

---

6. I explore this in depth in my doctoral work and in a recent publication (Todd 2014).

source of food is unavailable, if you have fish, you won't starve. It wasn't until *after* I had moved back to Scotland to write that I began to untangle my utilitarian understanding of the statement and began to see the fish pluralities she was referencing. This was not a lesson solely about food, but about the many manifestations and articulations of human-fish relations in Paulatuuq: as long as you have fish, you have stories, memories and teachings about how to relate thoughtfully with the world and its constituents. As long as you have fish (and other animals), you are nourished not only physically, but in a plurality of emotional, spiritual and intellectual ways as well. A world without fish is not only a hungry one, but one intellectually and socially bereft.

People I worked with in Paulatuuq demonstrated to me how they employ what Inuvialuit political leader and thinker Rosemarie Kuptana (cit.) calls the Inuit practice of 'principled pragmatism'. Working across both sameness and difference, Paulatuuq people employ strategies that incorporate elements of the Canadian State's wildlife scientific co-management system and Inuvialuit legal orders and thinking to assert the well-being of humans and fish alike. Employing this dynamic strategy, Paulatuuqmiut successfully shut down a government-mandated commercial fishery in a vital local watershed in the 1980s (cit.). The lives and stories of fish and people are tightly woven together in complex ways, and these relationships inform not just what might be glossed as cultural, religious, ontological or ecological concerns but also shape concrete, gritty, practical, fleshy lived legal-political (decolonial) realities as well.

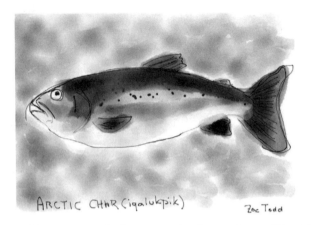

ARCTIC CHAR (iqalukpik)

Zoe Todd

By working outwards from particular and specific fish stories and memories that interlocutors shared with me in Paulatuuq, I was brought into a rich world of Indigenous legal-governance operating in dynamic ways across Canada. I was taught to see fish as non-human persons who consciously and actively respond to the human and non-human worlds around them. I was taught to understand land, climate/atmospheres, water and animals as sentient and knowing and to position my engagement with these agents ethically, reciprocally, and accountably. My presence as someone entangled in settler-colonial research systems was also made explicit, and forced me to question and engage with the uncomfortable question of what my role is (if any) as a southerner working in arctic Canada.

At the end of the day, I realized that I cannot work in the northern research industry while research in unceded Indigenous lands remains controlled, in large part, by southern non-Indigenous research institutions which operate under settler-colonial legal constructs (cit.). For now, I work in the territories where I grew up.
I make this choice so that I can renew and tend to the relationships to fish, people, lands and Indigenous laws that I was raised with but unable to 'see'.

Through my ethnographic experience, I was taught by Inuvialuit interlocutors to train my eyes, ears, heart and mind to honour implicit Indigenous laws long-obscured by the dominance of British and French laws employed by the Canadian State. I was also sensitized to the differences between laws, stories and relationships in Paulatuuq and those Métis teachings I grew up with on the green waters of Baptiste Lake in Alberta. Working within the frameworks of Indigenous legal orders resituates my duties from those that prioritise the academic-research industrial complex to a nuanced and careful negotiation of duties within, across and between Indigenous laws that centre and tend to land, water, fish, humans, and climate. For me, ethnography and anthropology remain fraught structures, processes and spaces. However, by tending to my duties to Inuit thinkers, and the philosophies they articulate (and intellectual labour they perform), and in tending to my legal-ethical duties as an Indigenous feminist working within the ongoing settler-colonial realities that shape Canada, I can slowly but insistently untangle some of the violences the academy reproduces in its iterations and interpretations of Indigenous philosophy.[7] *

---

7. For further reading on the negotiations of Indigenous philosophies within and outside of Euro-Western academic structures in North America, please review the works of John Borrows, Dwayne Donald, Sarah Hunt, Tracey Lindberg, Cutcha Risling Baldy, Erica Violet Lee, Val Napoleon, Audra Simpson, Kim TallBear, Eve Tuck, Vanessa Watts, Kyle Powys Whyte and other contemporary Indigenous thinkers working on these issues.

*In extension to this text, read Todd's *Fish, Kin and Hope: Tending to Water Violations in amiskwaciwâskahikan and Treaty Six Territory* (afterall.org), where she suggests that dinosaurs, flora and fauna—our fossil-kin embedded (documented) in oil—are being 'weaponised' by petroleum companies, as 'threats to our very existence as humans'.

Top
#141189 - 07/24/08 03:21 PM Re: The " bush" is not inert or neutral
[Re: Henry_Porter]
JohnN ☺   Living things may or may not be trying to kill you. The
Old Hand   universe doesn't care.

                -john

Registered: 10/10/01
Posts: 966
Loc: Seattle, WA

Previous Topic ⬤   Index ⬤   Next Topic ⬤   Page 1 of 3   1 2 3 >

The Companion Species Manifesto

Dogs, People, And Significant Otherness

From "Notes of a Sports Writer's Daughter"

*Ms. Cayenne Pepper continues to colonize all my cells—
a sure case of what the biologist Lynn Margulis calls sym-
biogenesis. I bet if you checked our DNA, you'd find some
potent transfections between us. Her saliva must have the
viral vectors. Surely, her darter-tongue kisses have been
irresistible. Even though we share placement in the phylum
of vertebrates, we inhabit not just different genera and
divergent families, but altogether different orders.*

*How would we sort things out? Canid, hominid; pet,
professor; bitch, woman; animal, human; athlete, handler. One of us has a microchip injected under her neck skin
for identification; the other has a photo ID California
driver's license. One of us has a written record of her ancestors for twenty generations; one of us does not know her
great-grandparents' names. One of us, product of
a vast genetic mixture, is called "purebred." One of us,
equally product of a vast mixture, is called "white."
Each of these names designates a racial discourse,
and we both inherit their consequences in our flesh.*

*One of us is at the cusp of flaming, youthful, physical
achievement; the other is lusty but over the hill. And we*

play a team sport called agility on the same expropriated Native land where Cayenne's ancestors herded merino sheep. These sheep were imported from the already colonial pastoral economy of Australia to feed the California Gold Rush forty-niners. In layers of history, layers of biology, layers of naturecultures, complexity is the name of our game. We are both the freedom-hungry offspring of conquest, products of white settler colonies, leaping over hurdles and crawling through tunnels on the playing field.

I'm sure our genomes are more alike than they should be. There must be some molecular record of our touch in the codes of living that will leave traces in the world, no matter that we are each reproductively silenced females, one by age, one by surgery. Her red merle Australian Shepherd's quick and lithe tongue has swabbed the tissues of my tonsils, with all their eager immune system receptors. Who knows where my chemical receptors carried her messages, or what she took from my cellular system for distinguishing self from other and binding outside to inside? We have had forbidden conversation; we have had oral intercourse; we are bound in telling story upon story with nothing but the facts. We are training each other in acts of communication we barely understand. We are, constitutively, companion species. We make each other up, in the flesh. Significantly other to each other, in specific difference, we signify in the flesh a nasty developmental infection called love. This love is a historical aberration and a naturalcultural legacy.

This manifesto explores two questions flowing from this aberration and legacy: (1) how might an ethics and politics committed to the flourishing of significant otherness be learned from taking dog–human relationships seriously; and (2) how might stories about dog–human worlds finally convince brain-damaged U.S. Americans, and maybe other less historically challenged people, that history matters in naturecultures?[...]

This is a story of biopower and biosociality, as well as of technoscience. Like any good Darwinian, I tell a story of evolution. In the mode of (nucleic) acidic millennialism, I tell a tale of molecular differences, but one less rooted in Mitochondrial Eve in a neocolonial *Out of Africa* and more rooted in those first mitochondrial canine bitches who got in the way of man making himself yet again in the Greatest Story Ever Told. Instead, those bitches insisted on the history of companion species, a very mundane and ongoing sort of tale, one full of misunderstandings, achievements, crimes, and renewable hopes. Mine is a story told by a student of the sciences and a feminist of a certain generation who has gone to the dogs, literally. Dogs, in their historical complexity, matter here. Dogs are not an alibi for other themes; dogs are fleshly material-semiotic presences in the body of technoscience. Dogs are not surrogates for theory; they are not here just to think with. They are here to live with. Partners in the crime of human evolution, they are in the garden from the get-go, wily as Coyote.

Prehensions

Many versions of process philosophies help me walk with my dogs in this manifesto. For example, Alfred North Whitehead described "the concrete" as "a concrescence of prehensions." For him, "the concrete" meant an "actual occasion." Reality is an active verb, and the nouns all seem to be gerunds with more appendages than an octopus. Through their reaching into each other, through their "prehensions" or graspings, beings constitute each other and themselves. Beings do not preexist their relatings. "Prehensions" have consequences. The world is a knot in motion. Biological and cultural determinism are both instances of misplaced concreteness—i.e., the mistake of, first, taking provisional and local category abstractions like "nature" and "culture" for the world and, second, mistaking potent consequences to be preexisting foundations. There are no pre-constituted subjects and objects, and no single sources, unitary actors, or final ends. In Judith Butler's terms, there are only "contingent foundations"; bodies that matter are the result. A bestiary of agencies, kinds of relatings, and scores of time trump the imaginings of even the most baroque cosmologists. For me, that is what companion species signifies.

My love of Whitehead is rooted in biology, but even more in the practice of feminist theory as I have experienced it. This feminist theory, in its refusal of typological thinking, binary dualisms, and both relativisms and universalisms of many flavors, contributes a rich array of approaches to emergence, process, historicity, difference, specificity, cohabitation, co-constitution, and contingency. Dozens of feminist writers have refused both relativism and universalism. Subjects, objects, kinds, races, species, genres, and genders are the products of their relating. None of this work is about finding sweet and nice—"feminine"—worlds and knowledges free of the ravages and productivities of power. Rather, feminist inquiry is about understanding how things work, who is in the action, what might be possible, and how worldly actors might somehow be accountable to and love each other less violently. [...]

IV. TRAINING STORIES

From "Notes of a Sports Writer's Daughter"
Marco, my godson, is Cayenne's god kid; she is his god dog. We are a fictive kin group in training. Perhaps our family coat of arms would take its motto from the Berkeley canine literary, politics, and arts magazine that is modeled after the Barb; namely, the Bark, whose masthead reads "Dog is my co-pilot." When Cayenne was twelve weeks old and Marco six years old, my husband, Rusten, and I gave him puppy-training lessons for Christmas. With Cayenne in her crate in the car, I would pick Marco up from school on Tuesdays, drive to Burger King for a planet-sustaining health food dinner of burgers, Coke, and fries, and then head to the Santa Cruz SPCA for our lesson.

*Like many of her breed, Cayenne was a smart and willing
youngster, a natural to obedience games. Like many of his
generation raised on high-speed visual special effects and
automated cyborg toys, Marco was a bright and motivated
trainer, a natural to control games.*

*Cayenne learned cues fast, and so she quickly plopped
her bum on the ground in response to a "sit" command.
Besides, she practiced at home with me. Entranced, Marco
at first treated her like a microchip-implanted truck for
which he held the remote controls. He punched an imaginary
button; his puppy magically fulfilled the intentions of his
omnipotent, remote will. God was threatening to become
our co-pilot. I, an obsessive adult who came of age in the
communes of the late 1960s, was committed to ideals of
intersubjectivity and mutuality in all things, certainly including dog and boy training. The illusion of mutual attention and communication would be better than nothing,
but I really wanted more than that. Besides, here I was the
only adult of either species present. Intersubjectivity does
not mean "equality," a literally deadly game in dogland;
but it does mean paying attention to the conjoined dance of
face-to-face significant otherness. In addition, control freak
that I am, I got to call the shots, at least on Tuesday nights.*

*Marco was at the same time taking karate lessons,
and he was profoundly in love with his karate master.
This fine man understood the children's love of drama,
ritual, and costume, as well as the mental-spiritual-bodily
discipline of his martial art. Respect was the word and the
act that Marco ecstatically told me about from his lessons.*

*He swooned at the chance to collect his small, robed self
into the prescribed posture and bow formally to his master
or his partner before performing a form. Calming his turbulent first-grade self and meeting the eyes of his teacher
or his partner in preparation for demanding, stylized
action thrilled him. Hey, was I going to let an opportunity
like that go unused in my pursuit of companion species
flourishing? "Marco," I said, "Cayenne is not a cyborg
truck; she is your partner in a martial art called obedience.
You are the older partner and the master here. You have
learned how to perform respect with your body and your
eyes. Your job is to teach the form to Cayenne. Until you
can find a way to teach her how to collect her galloping
puppy self calmly and to hold still and look you in the
eyes, you cannot let her perform the 'sit' command." It
would not be enough for her just to sit on cue and for him
to "click and treat." That would be necessary, certainly,
but the order was wrong. First, these two youngsters had to
learn to notice each other. They had to be in the same game.
It is my belief that Marco began to emerge as a dog trainer
over the next six weeks. It is also my belief that as he
learned to show her the corporeal posture of cross-species
respect, she and he became significant others to each other.*

*Two years later out of the kitchen window I glimpsed
Marco in the backyard doing twelve weave poles with
Cayenne when nobody else was present. The weave poles
are one of the most difficult agility objects to teach and to
perform. I think Cayenne and Marco's fast, beautiful
weave poles were worthy of his karate master.*

Positive Bondage

In 2002, the consummate agility competitor and teacher Susan Garrett authored a widely acclaimed training pamphlet called *Ruff Love*, published by the dog agility-oriented company Clean Run Productions. Informed by behaviorist learning theory and the resultant popular positive training methods that have mushroomed in dogland in the past twenty years, the booklet instructs any dog person who wants a closer, more responsive training relationship with her or his dog. Problems like a dog's not coming when called or inappropriate aggression are surely in view; but, more, Garrett works to inculcate attitudes informed by biobehavioral research and to put effective tools in the hands of her agility students. She aims to show how to craft a relationship of energetic attention that would be rewarding to the dogs and the humans. Non-optional, spontaneous, oriented enthusiasm is to be the accomplishment of the previously most lax, distracted dog. I have the strong sense that Marco has been the subject of a similar pedagogy at his progressive elementary school. The rules are simple in principle and cunningly demanding in practice; to wit, mark the desired behavior with an instantaneous signal and then get a reward delivered within the time window appropriate to the species in question. The mantra of popular positive training, "click and treat," is only the tip of a vast post-"discipline and punish" iceberg.

Emphatically, as the back of Garrett's tract proclaims in a cartoon, positive does not mean permissive. Indeed,

I have never read a dog-training manual more committed to near total control in the interests of fulfilling human intentions, in this case, peak performance in a demanding, dual species, competitive sport. That kind of performance can only come from a team that is highly motivated, not working under compulsion, but knowing the energy of each other and trusting the honesty and coherence of directional postures and responsive movements.

Garrett's method is exacting, philosophically and practically. The human partner must set things up so that the dog sees the clumsy biped as the source of all good things. Opportunities for the dog to get rewards in any other way must be eliminated as far as possible for the duration of the training program, typically a few months. The romantic might quail in the face of requirements to keep one's dog in a crate or tied to oneself by a loose leash. Forbidden to the pooch are the pleasures of romping at will with other dogs, rushing after a teasing squirrel, or clambering onto the couch—unless and until such pleasures are granted for exhibiting self-control and responsiveness to the human's commands at a near 100 percent frequency. The human must keep detailed records of the actual correct response rate of the dog for each task, rather than tell tales about the heights of genius one's own dog must surely have reached. A dishonest human is in deep trouble in the world of ruff love.

The compensations for the dog are legion. Where else can a canine count on several focused training sessions a day, each designed so that the dog does not make mistakes but instead gets rewarded by the rapid delivery of treats, toys, and liberties, all carefully calibrated to evoke and sustain maximum motivation from the particular, individually known pupil? Where else in dogland do training practices lead to a dog who has learned to learn and who eagerly offers novel "behaviors" that might become incorporated into sports or living routines, instead of morosely complying (or not) with poorly understood compulsions? Garrett directs the human to make careful lists of what the dog actually likes; and she instructs people how to play with their companions in a way the dogs enjoy, instead of shutting dogs down by mechanical human ball tosses or intimidating overexuberance. Besides all that, the human must actually enjoy playing in doggishly appropriate ways, or they will be found out. Each game in Garrett's book might be geared to build success according to human goals, but unless the game engages the dog, it is worthless.

In short, the major demand on the human is precisely what most of us don't even know we don't know how to do—to wit, how to see who the dogs are and hear what they are telling us, not in bloodless abstraction, but in one-on-one relationship, in otherness-in-connection.

There is no room for romanticism about the wild heart of the natural dog or illusions of social equality across the class Mammalia in Garrett's practice and pedagogy, but there is large space for disciplined attention and honest achievement. Psychological and physical

violence has no part in this training drama; technologies
of behavioral management have a starring role. I have
made enough well-intentioned training mistakes—some
of them painful to my dogs and some of them dangerous
to people and other dogs, not to mention worthless
for succeeding in agility—to pay attention to Garrett.
Scientifically informed, empirically grounded practice
matters; and learning theory is not empty cant, even if
it is still a severely limited discourse and a rough instrument. Nonetheless, I am enough of a cultural critic to
be unable to still the roaring ideologies of tough love in
high-pressure, success-oriented, individualist America.
Twentieth-century Taylorite principles of scientific
management and the personnel management sciences
of corporate America have found a safe crate around the
postmodern agility field. I am enough of a historian of
science to be unable to ignore the easily inflated, historically decontextualized, and overly generalized claims of
method and expertise in positive training discourse.

Still, I lend my well-thumbed copy of *Ruff Love* to
friends, and I keep my clicker and liver treats in my
pocket. More to the point, Garrett makes me own up to
the stunning capacity that dog people like me have to lie
to ourselves about the conflicting fantasies we project
onto our dogs in our inconsistent training and dishonest
evaluations of what is actually happening. Her pedagogy
of positive bondage makes a serious, historically specific
kind of freedom for dogs possible, i.e., the freedom to

live safely in multispecies, urban and suburban environments with very little physical restraint and no corporal punishment while getting to play a demanding sport with every evidence of self-actualizing motivation. In dogland, I am learning what my college teachers meant in their seminars on freedom and authority. I think my dogs rather like ruff tough love. Marco remains more skeptical.

Harsh Beauty

Vicki Hearne—the famous companion animal trainer, lover of maligned dogs like American Staffordshire Terriers and Airedales, and language philosopher—is at first glance the opposite of Susan Garrett. Hearne, who died in 2001, remains a sharp thorn in the paw for the adherents of positive training methods. To the horror of many professional trainers and ordinary dog folk, including myself, who have undergone a near-religious conversion from the military-style Koehler dog-training methods, not so fondly remembered for corrections like leash jerks and ear pinches, to the joys of rapidly delivering liver cookies under the approving eye of behaviorist learning theorists, Hearne did not turn from the old path and embrace the new. Her disdain for clicker training could be searing, exceeded only by her fierce opposition to animal rights discourse. I cringe under her ear pinching of my newfound training practices and rejoice in her alpha roll of animal rights ideologies. The coherence and power of Hearne's critique of both the clicker addicted and the rights besotted, however, command my respect and alert me to a kinship link. Hearne and Garrett are blood sisters under the skin.

The key to this close line breeding is their focused attention to what the dogs are telling them, and so demanding of them. Amazing grace, these thinkers attend to the dogs, in all these canines' situated complexity and particularity, as the unconditional demand of their relational practice. There is no doubt that behaviorist trainers and Hearne have important differences over methods, some of which could be resolved by empirical research and some of which are embedded in personal talent and cross-species charisma or in the incommensurable tacit knowledges of diverse communities of practice. Some of the differences also probably reside in human pigheadedness and canine opportunism. But "method" is not what matters most among companion species; "communication" across irreducible difference is what matters. Situated partial connection is what matters; the resultant dogs and humans emerge together in that game of cat's cradle. Respect is the name of the game. Good trainers practice the discipline of companion species relating under the sign of significant otherness.

Hearne's best-known book about communication between companion animals and human beings, *Adam's Task*, is ill titled. The book is about two-way conversation, not about naming. Adam had it easy in his categorical labor. He didn't have to worry about back talk; and God, not a dog, made him who he was, in His own image, no less. To make matters harder, Hearne has to worry about conversation when human language isn't the medium, but not for reasons most linguists or language philosophers would give. Hearne likes trainers' using ordinary language in their work; that use turns out to be important to understanding what the dogs might be telling her, but not because the dogs are speaking furry humanese. She adamantly defends lots of so-called anthropomorphism, and no one more eloquently makes the case for the intention-laden, consciousness-ascribing linguistic practices of circus trainers, equestrians, and dog obedience enthusiasts. All that philosophically suspect language is necessary to keep the humans alert to the fact that somebody is at home in the animals they work with.

Just who is at home must permanently be in question. The recognition that one cannot know the other or the self, but must ask in respect for all of time who and what are emerging in relationship is the key. That is true for all true lovers, of whatever species. Theologians describe the power of the "negative way of knowing" God. Because Who/What Is is infinite; a finite being, without idolatry, can only specify what is not, i.e., not the projection of one's own self. Another name for that kind of "negative" knowing is love. I believe those theological considerations are powerful for knowing dogs, especially for entering into a relationship, like training, worthy of the name of love.

I believe that all ethical relating, within or between species, is knit from the silk-strong thread of ongoing alertness to otherness-in-relation. We are not one, and being depends on getting on together. The obligation is to ask who are present and who are emergent. We know from recent research that dogs, even kennel-raised puppies, do much better than generally more brilliant wolves or human-like chimpanzees in responding to human visual, indexical (pointing), and tapping cues in a food-finding test. Dogs' survival in species and individual time regularly depends on their reading humans well. Would that we were as sure that most humans respond at better than chance levels to what dogs tell them. In fruitful contradiction, Hearne thinks that the intention-ascribing idioms of experienced dog handlers can prevent the kind of literalist anthropomorphism that sees furry humans in animal bodies and measures their worth in scales of similarity to the rights-bearing, humanist subjects of Western philosophy and political theory.

Her resistance to literalist anthropomorphism and her commitment to significant otherness-in-connection fuel Hearne's arguments against animal rights discourse. Put another way, she is in love with the crossspecies achievement made possible by the hierarchical discipline of companion animal training. Hearne finds excellence in action to be beautiful, hard, specific, and personal. She is against the abstract scales of comparison of mental functions or consciousness that rank organisms in a modernist great chain of being and assign privileges or guardianship accordingly. She is after specificity.

The outrageous equating of the killing of the Jews in

Nazi Germany, the Holocaust, with the butcheries of the animal-industrial complex, made famous by the character Elizabeth Costello in J. M. Coetzee's novel *The Lives of Animals*, or the equating of the practices of human slavery with the domestication of animals makes no sense in Hearne's framework. Atrocities, as well as precious achievements, deserve their own potent languages and ethical responses, including the assignment of priority in practice. Situated emergence of more livable worlds depends on that differential sensibility. Hearne is in love with the beauty of the ontological choreography when dogs and the humans converse with skill, face-to-face.. She is convinced that this is the choreography of "animal happiness," a title of another of her books.

In her famous blast in *Harper's* magazine in September 1991 titled "Horses, Hounds and Jeffersonian Happiness: What's Wrong with Animal Rights?" Hearne asked what companion "animal happiness" might be. Her answer: the capacity for satisfaction that comes from striving, from work, from fulfillment of possibility. That sort of happiness comes from bringing out what is within, i.e., from what Hearne says animal trainers call "talent." Much companion animal talent can only come to fruition in the relational work of training. Following Aristotle, Hearne argues that this happiness is fundamentally about an ethics committed to "getting it right," to the satisfaction of achievement. A dog and handler discover happiness together in the labor of training. That is an example of emergent naturecultures.

This kind of happiness is about yearning for excellence and having the chance to try to reach it in terms recognizable to concrete beings, not to categorical abstractions. Not all animals are alike; their specificity—of kind and of individual—matters. The specificity of their happiness matters, and that is something that has to be brought to emergence. Hearne's translation of Aristotelian and Jeffersonian happiness is about human–animal flourishing as conjoined mortal beings. If conventional humanism is dead in postcyborg and postcolonial worlds, Jeffersonian caninism might still deserve a hearing.

Bringing Thomas Jefferson into the kennel, Hearne believes that the origin of rights is in committed relationship, not in separate and preexisting category identities. Therefore, in training, dogs obtain "rights" in specific humans. In relationship, dogs and humans construct "rights" in each other, such as the right to demand respect, attention, and response. Hearne described the sport of dog obedience as a place to increase the dog's power to claim rights against the human. Learning to obey one's dog honestly is the daunting task of the owner. Her language remaining relentlessly political and philosophical, Hearne asserts that in educating her dogs she "enfranchises" a relationship. The question turns out not to be, What are animal rights, as if they existed preformed to be uncovered but, How may a human enter into a rights relationship with an animal? Such rights, rooted in reciprocal possession, turn out to be hard to dissolve; and the demands they make are life changing for all the partners.

Hearne's arguments about companion animal happiness, reciprocal possession, and the right to the pursuit of happiness are a far cry from the ascription of "slavery" to the state of all domestic animals, including "pets." Rather, for her the face-to-face relationships of companion species make something new and elegant possible; and that new thing is not human guardianship in place of ownership, even as it is also not property relations as conventionally understood. Hearne sees not only the humans but also the dogs as beings with a species-specific capacity for moral understanding and serious achievement. Possession—property—is about reciprocity and rights of access. If I have a dog, my dog has a human; what that means concretely is at stake. Hearne remodels Jefferson's ideas of property and happiness even as she brings them into the worlds of tracking, hunting, obedience, and household manners.

Hearne's ideal of animal happiness and rights is also a far cry from the relief of suffering as the core human obligation to animals. Human obligation to companion animals is much more exacting than that, even as daunting as ongoing cruelty and indifference are in this domain too. The ethic of flourishing described by the environmental feminist Chris Cuomo is close to Hearne's approach. Something important comes into the world in the relational practice of training; all the participants are remodeled by it. Hearne loved language about language; she would have recognized metaplasm all the way down.

Exercise

Windy.

How is it that I come to make something
(something "given", as they say, even now)
into words?

Windy. And cool.

Could the wind be training the trees?
No, for them, everything is finished before
    the wind comes.
Often people don't take up training either
because they think, and many are right,
    they are already finished products.

Have you lost your mind?
    Did it head for San Francisco?
And so it came to be. Became San Francisco.
Bitterly. Heavy. With iron-rimmed
cartwheels. Creaking

from the eastern edge to the western.
For reasons that are easy or uneasy to see
I think of European emigrants taking land.
As if it began to cloud over behind my brows.

27.8.03

something "given": something real, <u>existing inde-</u>
<u>pendently of me</u>. The word contains the notion
that the world was given by God. Just as in the word
gift [talent, ability *trans.*]: as if it were God-given.
As if my reaction were something akin to meddling.
This questionableness (see the question mark that
follows, also expressed in: **For reasons that are**
easy or uneasy to see) prepares the question
of how something so distant could preoccupy me.
trains: by tossing them to and fro.
finished products: they consider themselves
complete, finished [*gefertigt*, from *fertigen*,
to manufacture *trans.*]: they consider exercising
or practicing unnecessary.
In contrast, the privation of the emigrants comes
to mind.
cloud over: darkened—taken from the expression *be-*
wölkter Himmel [an overcast sky *trans.*]; as in the
German expression *bewölkte Stirn* [an overcast brow]

The Triumphing

of that which was triumphant. Of the standing of plants.
Out of the earth, into the air. Wisdom.

A balanced room, table top, cabinet leg.
Window frame, appearances, ceiling rafters.

The blossom, the fruit, the scattering.
The wilting, the retreat, a foundation of humus:

The—ocean wave—eternally same,
unsurpassed in its silence.

So look. So not to know, senseful.
Carpet of larch needles. Theirs. Theirs and always
theirs.

Along the edge of the street, the cut path, air and snow.
Dark as snow. Stars above pines too.

There were horses, and further blessed: now merely—
there were. Into the then past, our kin

moved, turned, post-diluvial histories.

22/23.11.03

The Triumphing//Of that which was triumphant.
That which stands/withstands, has triumphed over
that which preceded it. My purloining of this concept out of the human/animal realm expresses
what I want to say.
The standing of plants (*Pflanzenstand*). There is
a power which operates in the verb with<u>stand</u>, like
in the association with noble <u>standing</u> (*Adelsstand*):
equating it with the triumphant.
Wisdom. The—now emphasised—equation with human ability (as triumph).
A balanced room: human dwelling/the home—
balanced—stable, unvarying, at peace with itself,
neat—in its order **appearances:** on stage, but also
an association with conflict.
The blossom, the fruit, the scattering. Again the
plants, the scattering—when they scatter the seeds.
The wilting, the retreat—when they wilt in the autumn;
foundation of humus: here a touch of criticism towards the human: is it that we leave behind
a foundation of humus for our kind?
The—ocean wave—eternally same: however they are
not superior to us, they lack individual growth.
Unsurpassed in its silence: the verse shines because
it is irrefutable: critical-touch: <u>we</u> speak. ..
So look. So not to know: but we know **sensefully**
(*sinnsam*). They don't know, but they exist as if they
made sense. *Sittsam* (conforming to customs, mores)

is common = *gesittet* (mannered). A parallel formation. We view sense as our property. Thus, the word is related to both sides.

Carpet of larch needles: (Relates back to "foundation of humus")—And: the **eternally same. Theirs. Theirs and always theirs.** That which belongs to them. It repeats itself.

Along the edge of the street, the cut path, air and snow: The street knows a different form of continuation to repetition. **Along the edge:** The image of the forest forms: *Schneise* (path) a tree-free swathe cleared in the forest for forestry.

Dark as snow: Snow is dark inside, i.e. dark as such. Shift from this paradox-metaphor: **Stars above pines too.**

There were horses: Horses—draught horses, riding horses... I'm not thinking of horses for slaughter, but rather of their beauty and of them as human accomplishment and product of breeding, and further blessed—*selig*: as one used to speak of the dead: Uncle Albert (bless his soul)—here a little glimmer of the topos of a more beautiful past, and continuing on a matter-of-fact note: **now merely—there were—** the then past: the early history of humanity; **moved, turned**—turned away from there.

Our kin, us humans, **post-** after the Ice Age **histories.** Three long Os (*zogen*, *bogen*, *Historien*)— sonorous harmony to conclude the poem text.

Topic

pottering about: there you are things. Thieves.
Look out, otherwise your eye
just might exit you in the pottering about.

Eyesight: lantern. Standing outside.
Good for the night. And for foot traffic.

Your duodenum—here a loop, there a loop.
The supervision, the nerves? The department of nerves?

Nerves, nerves!
Left to their own devices!
In the faint wind there is a blustering about like the leaves.

20.12.07

Topic—the topic is://**pottering about** (*werkeln*): -
diminutive of the extinct word *werken* (to work), also
belittling: one does not complete a body of work by
pottering about. The eternal, fiddly labour of house-
work for instance: "the main thing that needs doing
is this, and that": **there you are things. Thieves.** You lose
yourself in the things, nothing of you is left, you
are their loot. **Thieves:** also functions as an exclamation:
Thieves! / **Look out, otherwise your eye** / **just might
exit you.** The cautionary observation implements itself,
transforms itself into movement.
might exit you—as it glances at the thing. Look out! Your
eye may just stay there! Moving on: **Eyesight: lantern.
Standing outside.** / **Good for the night.
And for foot traffic.** [*Augenlicht*—lit. eye-light, *trans.*]
continued association **Your duodenum—here a loop,
there a loop.//** **The supervision, the nerves?**
The department of nerves? The nerves had better be
careful. **Nerves, nerves!** // **Left to their own devices!**
thus they don't work. / Back outside: **In the faint wind,
there is a blustering about like the leaves.** The rhyming
of *Laub* with *Raub* [leaves with thieves, *trans.*] ends the
whole thing on a sarcastic note. *Brauselt* [blustering
about] instead of *braust* [blustering]—again belittling,
like *werkeln* above.

Translated by Charlotte Thießen & Joel Scott, and previously published in their
artiCHOKE #7

Afterword

P. 177

In the 1980s and 1990s, a general shift in the human sciences, glossed as "postmodernism," gave close attention to metaphor and representation, providing new life for the idea that cannibalism was nothing more than a colonizing trope and strategem, a calumny used by colonizers to justify their predatory behaviour... A common factor in the history of cannibal allegations is the combination of its denial among ourselves, and its attribution to those we wish to defame, conquer, and civilize. In an atmosphere of postcolonial guilt, denial about cannibalism was extended to denial on behalf of those we wished to rehabilitate and acknowledge as our equals.

P. 177 – 178

The figure of the cannibal, long used to construct racial boundaries, can now be called upon in projects to deconstruct them. The stigma is best countered when we look at our own behavior as well as the behavior of others. We may then be in a position to dislodge the savage-civilized dualism once essential to the formation of Western identity and Western forms of knowledge. We know, for example, that medicinal ingestion involving human flesh, blood, heart, skull, bone marrow, and other body parts was practiced widely throughout Europe from the sixteenth to the eighteenth centuries... The topic of cannibalism still elicits a compulsion by some to joke about the practice, and has nourished salacious accounts of Fore behaviour, [but] we are now better armed to respond to the call for philosophical housecleaning around the complexities of getting to know cannibals.

P. 172

The South Fore now say, without a sense of conflict, that they live with two religions. Ancestral songs at funerals are sung with heads bowed toward the earth, the ground from which the original Creative Beings emerged. Church hymns are sung with heads raised toward heaven...

NOAM CHOMSKY

Grammar, Mind and Body

A Personal View

WE CONSTANTLY HEAR that a failure of modern linguistics is that it hasn't provided a complete grammar of *any* language. One doesn't hear claims that modern science has failed because it hasn't provided a complete account of the mammalian visual system or the navigational system of bees. The reason for this goes back to the belief ('dogma' might be better) that the workings of the mind have to be transparent—for contemporary philosophy it's often a definition: something is in the mind if it's accessible to introspection (understandable doctrine but completely untenable).

It was thought traditionally—you can go back centuries—that the study of the mind would be easier than physics, because it's all open to you—all you have to do is 'look'. Well, you can learn a lot about language from a traditional or pedagogic grammar; but the reason for that is because you already know the answers to the most fundamental questions; and you know the answers because you are a human being and you have the human language capacity which enables you to acquire your language in the first place—from scattered and complex data—more or less organised and presented in something that's called 'a grammar' of the language.

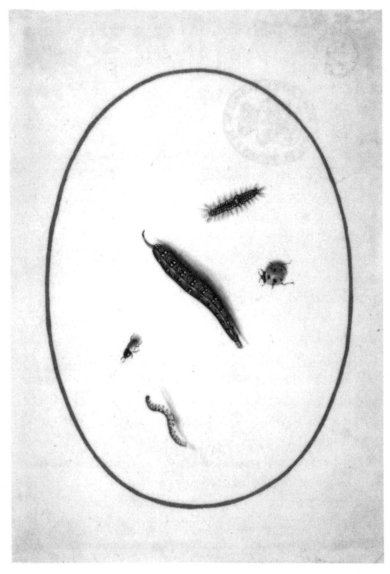

Caterpillars and insects, in transverse oval with gold edge, circa 1770.

It wouldn't be too far off the mark to suggest that
grammars are collections of idiosyncrasies: things
that you can't know just by being human. So you
have to pick them up from data. In a rather similar way:
if you have a manual teaching tennis, it won't go into
the instructions that you send from your motor-cortex
to your arm to lift up the racket; and a theory of motor
organisation is not going to care how you get your ball
past the opponent on the first serve. In general the scientific theories are almost *complementary* to the manuals
of instruction: they deal with different things. What
you don't care about for the manual of instruction
is what you do care about for the scientific theory.

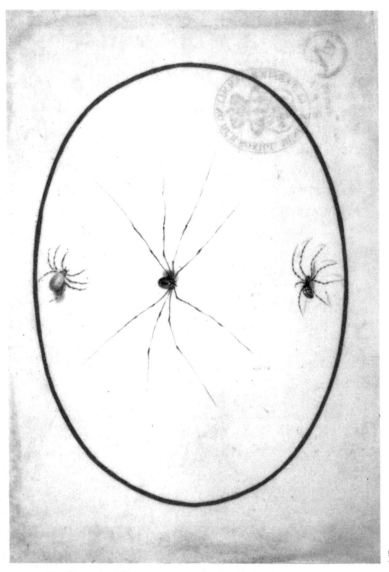

Two fleas and a tick, in transverse oval with gold edge, circa 1770.

On The Difference Between the *Ethics* and A Morality

NO PHILOSOPHER was ever more worthy, but neither was any philosopher more maligned and hated. To grasp the reason for this it is not enough to recall the great theoretical thesis of Spinozism: a single substance having an infinity of attributes, *Deus sive Natura*, all "creatures" being only modes of these attributes or modifications of this substance. It is not enough to show how pantheism and atheism are combined in this thesis, which denies the existence of a moral, transcendent, creator God. We must start rather from the practical theses that made Spinozism an object of scandal. These theses imply a triple denunciation: of "consciousness," of "values," and of "sad passions." These are the three major resemblances with Nietzsche. And already in Spinoza's lifetime, they are the reasons for his being accused of *materialism*, *immoralism*, and *atheism*.

1. A devaluation of consciousness (in favor of thought):
Spinoza the materialist.
Spinoza offers philosophers a new model: the body. He proposes to establish the body as a model: "We do not know what the body can do…" This declaration of ignorance is a provocation. We speak of consciousness

and its decrees, of the will and its effects, of the thousand ways of moving the body, of dominating the body and the passions—but *we do not even know what a body can do.*[1] Lacking this knowledge, we engage in idle talk. As Nietzsche will say, we stand amazed before consciousness, but "the truly surprising thing is rather the body…"

Yet, one of the most famous theoretical theses of Spinoza is known by the name of *parallelism*; it does not consist merely in denying any real causality between the mind and the body, it disallows any primacy of the one over the other. If Spinoza rejects any superiority of the mind over the body, this is not in order to establish a superiority of the body over the mind, which would be no more intelligible than the converse. The practical significance of parallelism is manifested in the reversal of the traditional principle on which Morality was founded as an enterprise of domination of the passions by consciousness. It was said that when the body acted, the mind was acted upon, and the mind did not act without the body being acted upon in turn (the rule of the inverse relation, cf. Descartes, *The Passions of the Soul*, articles 1 and 2). According to the *Ethics*, on the contrary, what is an action in the mind is necessarily an action in the body as well, and what is a passion in the body is necessarily a passion in the mind.[2] There is no primacy of one series over the other.

---

1. *Ethics*, III, 2, scholium.
2. *Ethics*, 111, 2, schol. (and II, 13, schol.).

What does Spinoza mean when he invites us to take the body as a model? It is a matter of showing that the body surpasses the knowledge that we have of it, *and that thought likewise surpasses the consciousness that we have of it*. There are no fewer things in the mind that exceed our consciousness than there are things in the body that exceed our knowledge. So it is by one and the same movement that we shall manage, if possible, to capture the power of the body beyond the given conditions of our knowledge, and to capture the power of the mind beyond the given conditions of our consciousness. One seeks to acquire a knowledge of the powers of the body in order to discover, *in a parallel fashion*, the powers of the mind that elude consciousness, and thus to be able to *compare* the powers. In short, the model of the body, according to Spinoza, does not imply any devaluation of thought in relation to extension, but, much more important, a devaluation of consciousness in relation to thought: a discovery of the unconscious, of an *unconscious of thought* just as profound as *the unknown of the body*.

The fact is that consciousness is by nature the locus of an illusion. Its nature is such that it registers effects, but it knows nothing of causes. The order of causes is defined by this: each body in extension, each idea or each mind in thought are constituted by the characteristic relations that subsume the parts of that body, the parts of that idea. When a body "encounters" another body, or an idea another idea, it happens that the two relations sometimes combine to form a more powerful whole, and sometimes one decomposes the other, destroying the cohesion of its parts. And this is what is prodigious in the body and the mind alike, these sets of living parts that enter into composition with and decompose one another according to complex laws.[3] The order of causes is therefore an order of composition and decomposition of relations, which infinitely affects all of nature. But as conscious beings, we never apprehend anything but the *effects* of these compositions and decompositions: we experience *joy* when a body encounters ours and enters into composition with it, and *sadness* when, on the contrary, a body or an idea threaten our own coherence. We are in a condition such that we only take in "what happens" to our body, "what happens" to our mind, that is, the effect of a body on our body, the effect of an idea on our idea. But this is only our body in its own relation, and our mind in its own relation, and the other bodies and other minds or ideas in their respective relations, and the rules according to which all these relations compound with and decompose one another; we know nothing of all this in the given order of our knowledge and our consciousness. In short, the conditions under which we know things and are conscious of ourselves condemn us *to have only inadequate ideas*, ideas that are confused and mutilated, effects separated from their real causes.[4]

---

3. Even the mind has a very large number of parts: cf. *Ethics*, II, 1 5.
4. *Ethics*, 11, 28, 29.

That is why it is scarcely possible to think that little children are happy, or that the first man was perfect: ignorant of causes and natures, reduced to the consciousness of events, condemned to under go effects, they are slaves of everything, anxious and unhappy, in proportion to their imperfection.

P. 180

For many decades, the Fore confronted a multitude of new objects and technologies, introduced by a regime of power whose personnel held different conceptions of life and death. A particular challenge for the Fore has been how to explain the disappearance of the disease that once endangered their survival. Most people said that kuru had disappeared with the arrival of the mission, the school, and the market – a set of coherences that seemed causal. Some said that sorcerers had turned to more profitable kinds of business, and most agreed that kuru would end when the last of the generation of old men had died, taking with them their special knowledge of kuru sorcery.

P. 179

In 1997, [Stanley] Prusiner was awarded the Nobel Prize for his finding that normally innocuous cellular proteins can convert their structures into pernicious conformations that damage nerve cells.

P. 179

...he described the elusive infectious agent as a "prion," until that time called a "slow virus"... Prions, Prusiner said, consisted of malformed proteins and nothing else. Moreover, prions might be inherited, transmitted through infection, or occur spontaneously.

P. 179

With the appearance of BSE in the United Kingdom in 1986... the kuru epidemic acquired new global relevance... Kuru provided the example of an epidemic thought to have resulted from consumption of an individual dying of sporadic Creutzfeldt-Jakob Disease, followed by the recycling of the infectious agent within the community as others developed the disease and were themselves consumed.

COLOPHON

'Recognition' is the fourteenth issue of
F.R.DAVID, published by twice-yearly
by

uh books
2/2 7 Newark Drive,
Glasgow G41 4QJ
wh@uhbooks.directory

with
KW Institute for Contemporary Art
Auguststraße 69 10117 Berlin

Editors: Will Holder and Scott Rogers
Typesetting: Will Holder
Management: Emmie McLuskey
Print: Tallinna Raamatutrükikoda
Edition: 1000
ISBN: 978-0-9957133-3-8

We are grateful to all authors,
publishers and estates for granting
permissions. All efforts have been
otherwise made to contact the
rightful owners with regards to
copyrights and permissions. Please
contact em@uhbooks.directory
with any requests or queries.

Many thanks to: all authors,
Dirk Cieslak, Cinenova, Mason
Leaver-Yap, Shirley Lindenbaum,
Kirsteen MacDonald, Karolin
Meunier, Tahani Nadim, Christian
Oldham, Other Feminist Readers,
Jaakko Pallasvuo, Elsa Richardson,
Jimmy Robert, William Rodwell,
Sarah Rose, Charlotte Thießen
& Joel Scott, Kristy Trinier,
The Estate of Ian White.

Previous page: Scott Rogers, *Endling*, 2015.
The texts, on pages throughout this issue,
are extracts of writings by the anthropologist
Shirley Lindenbaum [*Kuru Sorcery: Disease
and Danger in the New Guinea Highlands*,
second edition, expanded and updated. 1st
edition: 1978, 2nd edition: 2014, Routledge.]
The text—set in The Doves Type—was
installed in the same space as a hand-made
decoy of the extinct passenger pigeon.

Front cover: *Eat, prey, love*: "bald eagles
adopt baby red-tail hawk into their nest
in Canada. The chick was first seen [on
Vancouver Island], late May 2017—possibly
after one of the bald eagles raided a hawk's
nest to provide food for their young."
"Others believe a hawk laid its eggs in the
nest before the eagles arrived and the baby
hawk was the only [survivor] before being
adopted" [because] "it may have been the
bald eagle's maternal instinct that spurred
its change of heart." "'My guess is that this
little guy begged loud and hard for food—
not even thinking about the danger,' Bird
told the Sun." "Normally, bald eagles and
red-tailed hawks are nothing short of bitter
rivals." [Yet, this hawk] "is in excellent health
after being taken in, and now 'thinks he's
a bald eagle' [but] 'the bottom line is that
he was much smaller", [so] "They're going
to look at this little hawk and say 'I'm bigger
than you, you're weaker than me and I'm
going to just squeeze the life out of you and
start eating you,' Bird told the news station."
"June 28, 2017: The red-tailed hawk chick
[…] took its first flight last Friday, travelling
about 30 metres from the nest it shares with
two adult eagles and three eaglets." […]
"7/16/17: LittleEagle (aka Spunky)
continues to thrive. He (she?) is still
being cared for by the parent eagles, and
has developed an eagle-like affinity for fish."

Back cover: from Ursula K. Le Guin,
*A Non-Euclidean View of California
as a Cold Place to Be* (1982)